The Sober Girl Society Handbook

An empowering guide to living hangover-free

MILLIE GOOCH

BANTAM PRESS

TRANSWORLD PUBLISHERS
Penguin Random House, One Embassy Gardens,
8 Viaduct Gardens, London sw11 7bw
www.penguin.co.uk

Transworld is part of the Penguin Random House group of companies
whose addresses can be found at global.penguinrandomhouse.com

First published in Great Britain in 2021 by Bantam Press
an imprint of Transworld Publishers

A CIP catalogue record for this book
is available from the British Library.

ISBN 9781787634121

Text design by Couper Street Type Co.
Typeset in 11.5/15pt Granjon LT Std by Jouve (UK), Milton Keynes
Printed and bound in Great Britain by Clays Ltd, Elcograf S.p.A.

The authorized representative in the EEA is Penguin Random House Ireland,
Morrison Chambers, 32 Nassau Street, Dublin D02 YH68

Penguin Random House is committed to a sustainable
future for our business, our readers and our planet. This book
is made from Forest Stewardship Council® certified paper.

Author note

Dear reader,

Though I hope this handbook can empower you to change your relationship with alcohol, it isn't, and should never be, a substitute for proper medical or psychological help. I am a writer, not a doctor, a therapist or an addiction professional, and if you believe that you might need extra help with your drinking then please be sure to speak to your doctor or check out the resources at the back of this book. Everything contained in this handbook comes from my personal experience and the experiences of those I have interviewed, but it may not be your experience.

For some people, simply quitting drinking can be dangerous and a detox of this kind should be carried out under medical supervision. Please consult your GP first before taking any of the advice from this book on breaking up with booze.

Lots of love,
Millie x

Patricia Amelia Bowen.
My beautiful Granny who
always said 'This too shall pass' but never got to
see that it actually did.
1929–2017

Contents

PART ONE

Breaking Up with Booze

Gin-dependent Women

Why is alcohol everywhere?

Hey, sister! Welcome to the Sober Girl Society. I for one am *so* glad you're here. My name is Millie Gooch (yep, my surname is also a slang word for the bit between a man's testicles and his anus), and if you want to come and say hi, or share the struggle of having a near-phallic surname, then you can find me on Instagram @milliegooch. I use she/her pronouns.

I set up SGS in 2018 to fulfil a desire to connect with like-minded women who were also embracing sobriety. Girls similar to me who didn't want to compromise on having fun and socializing, but who no longer felt alcohol was the faithful friend it once was. I wanted to create a place where women could discuss the best non-alcoholic wines, muse on the potential pitfalls of sober dating, and show the world that being alcohol-free is anything but boring!

I hate to come straight out with the formalities, but before we get stuck in I'd like us to agree to a few pledges so that we have a mutual understanding. It's common to have a complex relationship with alcohol, so I hope this helps those of you who might be approaching this book with mixed feelings or slight trepidation.

I, the reader . . .

💜 Will acknowledge that everything I am being told in this book comes from a place of love and *not* judgement. The author of this book has been there, done that and got the wine-stained T-shirt to prove it.

💜 Will not worry about labels. 'Sober', 'sober curious', 'alcohol-free', 'non-drinker', 'mindful drinker': it doesn't matter at this point/if ever. All I am doing is reading a book, learning some facts and considering some opinions. The only label I need is my name, and SGS isn't bothered if I want to drop that either.

💜 Will keep an open mind and acknowledge that a lot of what I am about to read might feel like listening to one friend trying to tell another friend that their partner is cheating on them. In fact, some parts of this book might make for uncomfortable reading, but this is good because my perceptions are being challenged and my horizons are being broadened. The truth can sometimes hurt, but then it will set me (alcohol-) free.

💜 Will not, under any circumstances, use this book as a coaster for a glass of wine, gin or any other alcoholic beverage.

💜 Will try to read as much as possible, even if I don't think it's relevant, because knowledge is power, and perhaps it might help me to understand the world and the struggles of others a little better. I will try not to skim read while watching Netflix, only to realize that I haven't taken anything in and then have to flick back a couple of pages.

♥ Will read this book loudly and proudly and not hide it away. I acknowledge that breaking the stigma around sobriety is important, and reading this book in the open, on a train or in a café, might help to change someone else's perceptions too.

♥ Will not be afraid to annotate this book, because highlighting is welcome in this house. A well-worn book is a well-loved book (but I will not take this to mean I should scribble all over my Kindle).

♥ Will know that while this book will help me to navigate a world without alcohol, it is really all about choice. Sober Girl Society doesn't believe that alcohol empowers us, but sobriety doesn't necessarily do that for us either. It is choosing what feels genuinely right for us as individual human beings that is empowering. Whatever relationship I decide to have with alcohol once I've read this book is completely up to me, but at least I'll have the facts.

♥ Will take this as my official trigger warning for the contents of this book, as some material might be difficult for me to read. For example, Chapter Four includes some discussion around the topics of self-harm and suicide, and in later chapters there are mentions of sexual assault and domestic violence. Because of the sensitive nature of everything being discussed, details of support helplines are included on pages 279–289. I promise to make use of them if I am struggling or feel affected by any of the issues raised.

♥ Will regularly acknowledge while reading this that I am an awesome, amazing and incredible human being who is trying my best, and that I am always welcome at the Sober Girl Society.

There we have it.

I'm not sure exactly what led you to pick up this book, but I'm going to take a stab that it's one of the following: you're questioning your relationship with alcohol; tired of feeling like shit; already sober; or you're one of my family members who has been politely coerced into buying it (sorry in advance for the swearing, Mum). Perhaps you're even hungover right now – in which case, go get yourself a Berocca and a sachet of rehydration salts. I'll wait right here.

Before I throw you in at the deep end, I think it's important to run over a few booze-related details for context, just so that we're all on the same page. Starting with the science!

What Is Alcohol?

The answer to this might seem fairly obvious, but how many of us would default to 'wine' or 'something that gets you trolleyed'? There are actually many different types of alcohol. The one we drink is ethanol, and it's worth noting that it's used in some hairsprays, paints, varnishes and hand sanitizers as well. It was also used as fuel when rockets were first developed.

Alcohol is a toxic and extremely addictive substance. It is highly diffusible across cell membranes and metabolized by most tissues, meaning its toxicity affects the majority of your organs, but especially your liver, where most of the alcohol metabolization happens. Alcohol can dehydrate you, irritate your digestive system, contribute to electrolyte imbalances, impact your immune system, throw off your blood sugar levels and have a detrimental effect on your sleep – all of which can contribute to that wonderfully painful state we've come to know as a hangover. Drinking alcohol can affect everything from your mental health to your risk of developing cancer. Basically, it isn't kale.

The Nineties and Boozy Britain

I was born in 1991, at the start of the decade when the Spice Girls reigned supreme and women – fresh off the second feminist wave of the sixties, seventies and eighties – decided to take back our power. We wanted to prove that whatever men could do we could do too, and sometimes do it even better. One of the first orders of business? Matching the guys when it came to drinking, and in 1994 the British press coined the term 'ladette'.

Ladette culture became a movement led by the likes of Zoe Ball and Denise van Outen (who are both now known for their sobriety stints), and whilst their raucous behaviour and unashamed drunken antics did some incredible work in breaking down gender stereotypes (something for which I am eternally thankful), it seems that the actual boozing of it all may have come at a price. In the UK, between 1991 and 2004, alcohol-related deaths in the female population doubled, and the binge-drinking and heavy smoking associated with ladette culture have since been cited for their role in everything from cancer and heart disease to addiction.[1]

Fast forward a few years and stylish stars such as Kate Moss (also sober these days) started 'getting mossed' and falling out of nightclubs, while on the other side of the pond we were shown Carrie and the gang sipping Cosmos in swanky Manhattan bars. All of which meant that alcohol quickly became seen as the ultimate marker of the empowered party girl who knew exactly what she wanted and didn't give a flying fuck what anyone else thought. For a very long time, that's exactly how I saw it too.

Millie vs. Alcohol

When it comes to drinking, I was a latecomer in British terms. Despite the fact that most of my school friends spent their weekends drinking White Lightning cider down the local park, I had very little experience of alcohol as a teenager. From the age of eight I was really into dancing, so rather than swigging on the swings, my weekends were spent either training or competing.

My first experience of being very drunk wasn't until I was seventeen. It was 2009, I'd just finished my exams, and had managed to sneak into a club in London using my friend's ID. I don't really remember a lot of that night, except being held up on the dance floor by my friend Tom because I couldn't stand unassisted. Buried deep in the Facebook archives are photos from that night, of me with red lipstick smeared all over my face. They weren't my pictures, though, because I managed to lose my digital camera while we were out. That sort of behaviour was probably a sign of things to come.

A few months after that outing, I turned eighteen. It was the same day I got my A-level results, and I celebrated the fact that I was off to university and legally allowed to drink booze by ordering a pitcher of Blue Lagoon at the local Wetherspoon's at 10 a.m. (For anyone who isn't familiar with the drink, Blue Lagoon is a fluorescent mix of blue Curaçao, vodka, lime cordial and lemonade. I tell you this so that you can imagine how disgusting it was, not so that you can replicate it!)

Over the course of the next six months I moved to Brighton to study English at the University of Sussex, got myself a job promoting club nights and threw myself into the university drinking culture at what one might best describe as an 'alarming rate'. Before I knew it, I'd gone from being a girl who had been drunk once in her life to a girl who was drunk three or four nights a week minimum. From fresher bar crawls to £1.50 triple vodka Red Bulls (of which I would buy two, and tip them into a pint glass to make six shots), drinking became everything to me.

Having been somewhat of a goody-two-shoes, drinking felt like unleashing a carefree siren who didn't worry about what anyone thought of her. Drinking made me feel cooler, it made me feel sexier, it made me feel pretty invincible, and it became a cloak of confidence that I'd wrap around me. Once Millie the studious trained dancer, I was now Millie the loud-mouth party girl, and I loved it. I drank as much as I wanted, whenever I wanted, and decided that that would mean 'a lot' and 'often', flitting between being thrown out of nightclubs and drinking wine in the living room of our student house.

Of course, as a young single woman finding out how best to adult, *Sex and the City* became my bible – I'd never seen it before university, but my best friend, Emma, had the boxset. Sometimes, in our first year, we'd squeeze into my single bed and would fall asleep watching it. We'd wake up to the title theme playing between episodes, and Carrie Bradshaw repeatedly asking if all men were cheats. Despite its flaws, *SATC* reinforced the notion that drinking made me independent, drinking was powerful, and drinking was the only way to bond with my best friends. It confirmed to me the narrative that, as a young single woman, I was supposed to drink, and it confirmed that it didn't matter if I was happy or sad, cocktails were always the answer.

You can imagine my mixed feelings when I found out recently that Kristin Davis (who played Charlotte York) has actually been sober since the age of twenty-two, meaning that during filming she wouldn't have drunk a single Cosmopolitan, even off-screen. An interview with Sarah Jessica Parker also revealed that the Cosmos were made of watered-down cranberry juice, and the on-set substitute for champagne was ginger ale. Though I am under no illusion that *SATC* is anything but a fictional television show, I also know full well that my subconscious bought into the story that it was promoting – that booze was an essential part of female adulting.

At the height of its popularity, *Geordie Shore* was another television staple in our university house, and we often raced back home from lectures in time to watch it. We frequently sat open-mouthed as the female leads – Charlotte, Vicky, Sophie and Holly – led the charge for going out and getting blind drunk (or 'mortal' as they termed it), flashing their bits to the camera and wreaking havoc on the city of Newcastle. I knew their behaviour was out of hand, but I loved how fearless and outrageous they were.

What I failed to process was that despite being encouraged to neck back drinks, ultimately the cast's safety was still of paramount importance because it was a TV show – there was always a cameraman who would escort them home or a security guard who would break up their fights. I didn't have any of those safety mechanisms in place and started ending up in locations where I really didn't want to be, doing things I really didn't want to do.

Pretty soon my speciality became blackout binge-drinking. Towards my third year at university, my behaviour got steadily worse, and the situations I put myself in became more erratic and dangerous. When all my friends started taking their studies more seriously, I started throwing more strops because they would refuse to come out and get shit-faced with me. The only thing I wanted to take more seriously was drinking.

When I graduated, my boozing showed no signs of slowing down. I took my blackout binge-drinking habits with me to my internship in PR, and then on to my career in journalism. It was during this time that I realized pretty quickly that my relationship with alcohol was becoming a little problematic, but it didn't feel like anything out of the ordinary for a twenty-something working in London – there were simply a few incidents when I'd embarrass myself at work events, end up at train stations miles away from my house, and would have to face the office the next day when I'd turn up late, sporting a Pret bacon roll and a rather sheepish look.

At that point, I began to realize that I was probably a few drunken work nights away from a meeting with HR, so I began turning down invitations for drinks with colleagues of a week night. Instead, I would put all my energy into living for the weekend. I knew my friends were starting to grow tired of my drunken antics, but at least they couldn't fire me from my job. It meant that rather than spreading my alcohol consumption across the course of a week, I would just drink it all in one go. I told myself I deserved it – it had been a long week, it was my treat, and a tote bag told me I was 'gin-credible'!

My drinking continued in this vein for the next few years – a cycle of getting hammered on Friday and Saturday nights, then spending Sunday recovering in a pit of my own anxious shame. It was at this point that some of my more serious problems began. My mental health took a nosedive, and I began to notice that I was feeling down a lot more often than usual, despite the fact that I appeared to have everything going for me.

The 'hangxiety' – also known as 'the fear' – started to become worse than any physical symptoms of my hangover, and these periods of anxiety became longer and more pronounced. Rather than resting and recuperating at the weekend, I spent the majority of the time fretting that I'd upset everyone, worrying that no one liked me, beating myself up for not being able to drink 'responsibly', and feeling generally like a terrible human being.

I knew that I wasn't living the life I wanted, but quite honestly, I had no idea where to begin with fixing it. At that time I couldn't even lift my head from the pillow. Sometimes it felt like the effort it would take to find a solution to my unhappiness was too much, whereas I knew that drinking would cheer me up instantly. Rather than looking to the things that might make me happier in the long term, which seemed like an exhausting and overwhelming prospect, short-term fixes such as alcohol and cigarettes just felt easier.

Throughout all of this I would constantly reassure myself that my drinking was normal. After all, I could happily go the rest of the week without touching a drop, and it wasn't like I was pouring vodka on my breakfast cereal. I told myself I was just a millennial party girl, like the ones on *Geordie Shore*, and that I was living life as a ladette – young, carefree and doing exactly what I wanted. Except deep down, it felt as if the game had changed. If anything, I now had too many cares, and drinking felt less like something I wanted and more like something I needed. Something that perked me up, something that gave me confidence, and something that hushed all my insecurities. Without it, I felt boring and awkward and constantly in my head.

Towards the end of 2017, I broke up with my boyfriend of six years for the second time, and I took it particularly badly. I used it as my excuse to drink more, mainly because that's how I'd been taught to fix a broken heart – drink, dance and repeat. Except this time it didn't work – it made things worse. My work rule went out the window because any excuse to drink was now a valid one, so I flitted between feeling drunk, embarrassed, shameful, relatively sad and downright Eeyore.

When Valentine's weekend 2018 rolled around, and most people were looking forward to cuddling up on the sofa or staring longingly at each other over the dinner table, I was getting so out of it that the only thing I remember is walking into a nightclub and then everything going dark.

When I woke up the next day, I was filled with a familiar wave of dread and sickness. Not just because of the poison I'd shovelled in to my poor body, but because I was riddled with anxiety. My friends told me about the embarrassing things I'd done, in their usual flippant tone, and I had texts in my phone from someone called Tommy, telling me how drunk I was. If you had put Tommy in front of me that morning, I couldn't have picked him out of a line-up.

This might be the point in the book when you expect me to divulge my rock-bottom story – the shocking tale, the wake-up call – but that hangover was just like all the others. However, as I lay in bed I used a free monthly credit to download and listen to an audiobook I'd heard about a few months before: Catherine Gray's *The Unexpected Joy of Being Sober*.

That morning – 11 February 2018 – I cried tears of sadness and laughter while I listened to Cath talk about her relationship with alcohol. I realized that day that my drinking was a ticking time bomb. Catherine's life had so many parallels with my own, only she was a few years older, so I devoured her story as if she were the Ghost of Christmas Future. After I'd finished, I declared once and for all that I was never drinking again.

As I've mentioned, it certainly wasn't the worst hangover I'd ever experienced, but it *was* just one more time of waking up feeling ashamed, anxious, and sick and tired of my own shit, and I finally recognized that there's more to life than being hungover. I'd also like to explain that it definitely wasn't as easy as merely listening to an audiobook and, just like that, I never fancied alcohol again. There's a lot of work that goes into sobriety, as you will soon discover.

I do have a slight problem with the concept of rock bottom as a motivation to make a change. The idea that you have to have suffered a catastrophic fall from grace before you realize that something is bad for you. The idea that you have to wait until it's almost too late before you consider altering your behaviour. People constantly tell me, 'You weren't that bad', but by that logic, should I have kept drinking until I was? The point is, if you see a fire taking hold, you put it out. You don't wait until the blaze is so big that it burns down your house before taking action.

There will probably be people who'll say that I shouldn't be the one to write this book – that my stories are tame, and that I haven't been to the darkest depths of the murky underwater, but that really is the whole point. I am here to tell you that you don't need to hit a stereotypical rock bottom as depicted on screen. You don't need to wait until the world is falling apart around you. You can get off the ride any time you want. You don't need to wait until it's all gone to shit.

Make no mistake, even if you've experienced what you believe to be your version of a rock bottom, even if it feels like your world *is* falling apart, you are still so welcome here. Sober Girl Society is a ship that we're all on together, sailing against one big boozy tide. No matter what point in your drinking journey you're at – if you've decided to question it or stop entirely, we've got you! Most importantly, you don't need to justify yourself to anyone. Drinking problems do not materialize overnight – they are gradual and creep up on you. When people ask me if I stopped drinking because I had a problem, I tell them yes, but follow up with, 'But had I continued, I would've had a much bigger one.'

In an attempt to show you that alcohol doesn't need to ruin your life in order to still be a very obvious problem and obstacle that prevents you from living your best version of it, I will divulge some of my drinking stories, ranging from the tame and mildly embarrassing to the scary and slightly shameful. Rather than one big 'Aha!' moment, these are the interactions with alcohol that culminated in my decision to go sober. I'm sure there will still be people that, by comparison, have done far worse, and I'm OK with that. I am forever grateful that I made a decision that means my stories will never be scarier or more anxiety-inducing than the ones that follow here.

♥ The time I got so drunk on a night out in Brixton that
I snapped one of the straps on my shoe. It meant they were
no longer wearable and I had to commute back to Kent from

London in bare feet. The night was still young, so my friend Tasha volunteered to take me home so that the rest of my friends could stay out. It's worth noting that at this point I didn't know Tasha very well at all. Apparently, when we got on the tube, I had an absolute meltdown and tried to get off at every stop. Tasha's since told me that she tried to pin me down but I had weirdly superhuman strength. The other passengers looked at her like she'd just kidnapped me, and I kept yelling that she had to let me off the train.

♥ The time I woke up with seventy-four missed calls after drunk me decided to leave the club without telling everyone and go home to bed. My friends were convinced I'd been abducted until my mum confirmed I was, in fact, sound asleep at home.

♥ The time I reversed this scenario and woke up to fourteen dialled calls to someone I'd kissed once who then never spoke to me again.

♥ The time I vommed in my mouth on the tube to work after a Christmas Tequila Tuesday session with my friends.

♥ The time I woke up with no recollection of how I'd got home after another Tequila Tuesday, only strange flashbacks of me crying on a street corner. My Uber history showed the journey was terminated, and when I googled the postcode where it said I'd been dropped off, the street view looked like the place from my visions. To this day I have no idea how I got home from there, having made no cash withdrawals. It was too far to have walked, and was hours after I first left the pub.

♥ The time I came to, mid-blackout, and realized I was having sex with someone. That is a weird sentence, which I never thought I would write. I just remember being relieved that I recognized him as one of my friend's friends.

♥ The time I was out with friends in Bournemouth and, after we'd all come home, we were drunkenly messing around in our hotel bathroom. I fell backwards into the bath tub, hit my head on the tap and knocked myself out. My friends told me I was out cold and that they genuinely thought I was dead.

♥ The time my friend told me a very big secret but stressed she didn't want anyone else to know yet – she wanted to be the one to tell people. A week later, when I bumped into an old school friend, I drunkenly told her and news spread pretty fast. At the time, I didn't take any responsibility for my actions, and I never even apologized, out of shame. E – I am so sorry, I think about it at least once a day.

♥ The time the lights came on in a nightclub and I refused to go home, so my friend had to ask the bouncer to escort me outside. When I refused again, he dragged me out in a headlock that I somehow managed to escape, and I ran back into the club. In the end, he practically carried me out in a fireman's lift.

♥ The time I told my friends that I hated them, and that the day Emma died would be the best day of my life (it would actually be one of the worst FYI).

I genuinely have hundreds of these stories. I have upset people, hurt both myself and others. Truth be told, I'm surprised I have any friends left. So the message still stands: you do not have to wait until drinking has taken everything from you before you remove it from your life. You do not have to hit rock bottom, you can hit many rock middles and swim to the surface before the current drags you under.

Alcohol vs. Us

Fast forward even further to right now and alcohol is our hottest accessory. If we're not drinking it then we're thinking about drinking it, and if we're not drinking it or thinking about drinking it, then we're buying T-shirts and celebratory cards that send our friends well-wishes for a 'gin-tastic day' or a birthday that's 'as bubbly as champagne'. Our Christmas jumpers say 'prosec-ho-ho-ho', our mugs say 'G & Tea', while 'rosé all day' is our millennial-girl motto. Brunch, you say? Only if it's bottomless.

But what I have realized, in over three years of sobriety, is that everything about our relationship with alcohol is fraught with irony. Let me be clear, these observations are not meant to sound judgemental – for over twenty years I was, as Catherine Gray puts it, 'plugged into the alcohol matrix'. And when alcohol is so ubiquitous, it's near impossible not to get swept up in the glamorous advertising and narrative that booze is the ultimate fun juice. But now that I have metaphorically unplugged, these ironies are more obvious to me than ever.

Unfortunately, when it comes to talking about alcohol, if you start banging on about the benefits of sobriety and questioning the norms of our drinking culture or the industry that perpetuates it, then you're branded as a judgemental puritan on a high horse. So, to be clear, I'm genuinely allergic to horses and I'm just offering up some thoughts.

Isn't It Ironic . . . Don't You Think?

Social media is awash with voices, activists and individuals who are making some pretty epic changes in the world, for the better. But while conversations around feminism, mental health, social injustice, inequality, wellness and politics are all widening in their scope, one topic is consistently being glossed over. Ironically, it's a topic that feeds into every single one of those issues. It is, of course, alcohol.

In recent years, we have become a nation that is obsessed with checking and scrutinizing our food labels. We regularly shun gluten and dairy, we've made both sugar and carbs our enemies, and we're going vegan and paleo. We shop in Whole Foods and we practically vomit at the thought of ingesting something that isn't organic – but we don't question the fact that we're washing down our food with the same toxic substance we pump into our cars.

We might have green juice for breakfast, but we'll drink poison for dinner and show it off to the world. In fact, the hashtag #wineoclock features in over 2.7 million posts on Instagram, and #alcohol a staggering 11.1 million. The booze industry has, of course, caught up with our love of labels, and has responded to demand from those attempting to live a more conscious lifestyle by making a big push with products such as organic beer and biodynamic wine. Influencers with young fan bases plug alcohol, celebs peddle their own brands of it and, much like the iPhone, the newest model is never enough. When regular gin doesn't cut it, we move on to pink gin and craft gin and rhubarb gin and unicorn shimmer gin that twinkles when you puke it back up. But it doesn't matter how fancy your booze is, your health risks in consuming it are still the same. Alcohol is still carcinogenic, whether it's vegan or not.

Then, of course, there's the recent surge of 'wellness meets wasted'. Yoga is no longer just happy baby and tree poses, it's Vino & Vinyasa, or Yin & Gin. Quite frankly, it's counter-productive. Wellness websites are flooded with recipes for vitamin-packed cocktails to boost our immune system, but it seems no one has told these platforms that alcohol depletes vitamin stores in our body and weakens our immunity.

Even some of the biggest platforms and people we turn to for our information on wellness and healthy living don't seem to be in any hurry to point the finger at the fizz. Rather than acknowledging the benefits of cutting back on booze, the internet seems to be in favour of showcasing hangover cures ranging from IV drips to umeboshi (a type of Japanese plum harvested when the fruit acids are at their peak and then salt-pickled). While I'm sure you'll agree how practical and affordable these options are, I can tell you now that the only proven hangover cure is not to drink in the first place.

Alcohol doesn't just blur the wellness conversation, it impacts the mental health one too. It's been proved that alcohol can have some seriously negative consequences for our mental health, and we are just as bad at failing to address the issue during these discussions. Having spoken about alcohol and its effect on our emotional wellbeing pretty much every day since 2018, I often feel like I'm screaming into an abyss when I see mood-boosting cocktail menus and gin brands trying to drive sales by offering to donate a percentage of their profits to mental health charities.

The alcohol industry is consistently cited as one of the most environmentally harmful, but while we've invested in every reusable beverage container going, and branded anyone who doesn't use a metal straw a complete heathen, we barely mention alcohol in conversations around sustainability. Nor do we acknowledge the tonnes of unrecyclable material it generates. The Scotch whisky industry alone produces 500,000 tonnes of solid waste every year and 1.6 billion litres of waste liquids.[2]

Now more than ever we're gunning for autonomy and self-expression. We're in favour of people dressing how they choose and living how they want. We're supporting people in their pursuit to truly be their authentic selves. But non-drinkers? We dismiss them as no fun – they're boring. We're rising up against systems that tell us what to do and how to be, yet we rarely mention what a great act of defiance it is to choose not to drink in a world that profits from making people (especially women) feel like we should. Similarly, we're more body positive than ever, but when it comes to our personalities we are carefully curating ourselves to be more exciting, less inhibited. We're using alcohol to ease our anxiety when it's generally proven to make us *more* anxious.

We're politically savvy and profess to love our National Health Service despite the fact that alcohol-related illness and accidents costs the NHS £3.5 billion each year. One in ten people in a hospital bed are alcohol-dependent, and one in five are using alcohol 'harmfully', such as binge-drinking.[3] Even light-to-moderate drinking can increase your risk of developing life-threatening diseases such as breast cancer. In 2020, during the Covid-19 pandemic and UK lockdown, a time when looking after our health should have been a national priority, sales of alcohol (which weakens your immune system, leaving you more susceptible to contracting viruses) rocketed by a third.

The good news is that we've reached a tipping point with cigarettes, often the firm friend of alcohol. Once a product where certain brands were doctor-recommended, great strides have been made in recent years to dissuade everyone – but especially teens – from smoking. Unbranded packaging, graphic health warnings and a ban on menthol flavours have all contributed towards an enlightenment when it comes to the real dangers of smoking cigarettes, such as cancer.

But hang on, alcohol is linked to cancer too! Yet we stack it in supermarkets and department stores in pride of place. The bottles are like beautiful ornaments, and some of them even contain flecks of gold. They're brightly coloured, sleek as hell, and many of them appeal massively to young adults. Would we still buy the bottles if they were identical, plain, with just the word 'wine' written on them? Would we still give them as presents if they showed nothing but the word 'gin' and a picture of a woman with a mastectomy scar? Perhaps not.

Interestingly, there's another similar double standard: when you give up smoking people will congratulate you and tell you they're proud of you, but when you give up drinking the reaction is far from comparable. As the saying in the sober community goes, 'Alcohol is the only drug that you have to justify not taking.' And that is the most important point: alcohol is a drug.

In 2009, Professor David Nutt was fired as the government's chief drugs adviser, and he believes this was a result of his claim on national radio that alcohol was the most harmful drug in the UK. The rationale was this: alcohol warrants this position not just because of the harm it does to the individual, but because of the harm it does to society, including everything from crime rates and hospital bills to family conflict and environmental damage. Smoking, for example, doesn't fuel a lot of everyday crime, and there isn't a direct correlation with a dramatic rise in domestic violence, yet we've demonized it far more than booze. We've locked it away out of public sight and officially branded it 'uncool'.

Over the course of this book, I hope to give you the facts about booze and, more importantly, debunk some myths about sobriety. I hope to empower you with the tools and tips you need to change your relationship with alcohol *if you want to* (because remember, it's all about choice), and by the end who knows, you might even feel a fire in your belly to advocate for real change when it comes to all things ethanol-soaked. Not just for yourself but for others too.

It's at this point that I'd like to acknowledge that I am a straight, white, cis-gender female. I appreciate the privileged circumstances in which I've been able to embrace my sobriety. While we'll be discussing how alcohol impacts different people and the effects it can have across society as a whole, this book is founded in my own reality and largely draws from my own experience. It also comes from the view of someone brought up in an alcohol-centric western culture, so while I recognize that there are, of course, plenty of teetotal cultures, this book is a guide to ditching booze when 'not drinking' could outwardly be seen as a deviation from your norm.

Finally, I'd just like to say how lovely it is to have you here. Thank you for showing up, thanks for being open to new ways of thinking, and thank you for not immediately throwing this book in the bin *fingers crossed*.

Welcome to the Sober Girl Society <3

2

Independent Women

The curious case of the decline in drinking

N ow that you're fully initiated, it's time to get to the good stuff and showcase what this book is really all about – sobriety. This chapter is your beginner's guide: where you'll learn the lingo; find out what could be holding you back from making a change; discover the answers to my most frequently asked questions; and start to understand where you can possibly begin to change your relationship with alcohol for good.

We'll start with the epic news: a revolution is happening and the numbers seem to suggest that drinking habits are changing. In fact, the most recent stats show that nearly a third of 16–24-year-olds don't drink at all.[1] Could it be that sobriety's popularity amongst the younger generation means that going alcohol-free has finally become 'cool'?

When I started the Sober Girl Society back in 2018, there were very few online communities for sober women – particularly millennial ones who wanted to stop drinking and start living. But it seems the tide is turning. There are now AF (alcohol-free) and NA (non-alcoholic) bars, clubs, events and festivals popping up everywhere, and an absolute boom in alcohol-free beverages.

This isn't to say that the majority of people are going teetotal, but since 2005 the overall volume of alcohol consumed in the UK has fallen, as has the amount drinkers report they consume,[2] which suggests more people than ever are cutting down, taking longer periods of abstinence, joining in the dry months and becoming 'sober curious', a phrase that you've more than likely heard but might not be sure what it even means . . .

What Is Being Sober Curious?

Coined by author Ruby Warrington in her 2019 book of the same name, 'sober curious' is a term that has come to define the emerging mindful-drinking movement. The actual explanation of what sober curiosity means, however, has become a little confused. While some people take it to mean being curious about becoming a full-time non-drinker, Ruby herself describes it as questioning everything about your relationship with alcohol – including the way that we, as a society, view and consume it.

Rather than having to declare yourself a non-drinker, sober curious can be a permanent state in which you still drink on rare occasions, but generally become more aware of the motivations behind your drinking and aim to change your relationship with alcohol in a much more positive way.

For the record, sober-curious readers are absolutely welcome here, but whenever we speak about sobriety in this book, we are talking about good old-fashioned, teetotalling abstinence. Personally, I don't believe that you can reap 100 per cent of the magical benefits sobriety has to offer unless you ditch alcohol completely, but I do think that a sober-curious mindset is still a zillion times better than being caught in a perpetual cycle of binge-drinking and hangovers.

So Why Choose Teetotal?

If sober curiosity is such a big thing, you might be wondering why I've taken more of an all-or-nothing stance on my relationship with alcohol. For me, it's simple: I find moderation both exhausting and unattainable. Whenever I tried to cut back on my drinking, I had to make rules, such as having a maximum of three drinks, not drinking Monday to Wednesday, only drinking spirits, never drinking shots, not drinking after midnight, and only drinking at special events like weddings, birthdays or bottomless brunches (the latter hardly being the optimum setting for mindful drinking). I know I'm not the only one who found it difficult to cut back – many members of SGS have shared with me stories of their failed attempts at finding the elusive 'middle ground'.

These restrictions and complex regulations often made me feel like I was constantly tying myself up in knots, and I began to spend as much time thinking about my drinking as I did doing any drinking. It's important to understand that alcohol affects the part of your brain responsible for making rational decisions, so however much you intend to stick to your rules, three drinks in and you won't have the same willpower or resolve to abide by them as you would sober.

You'll know what I'm talking about if you've ever found yourself saying, 'I'm only having a couple tonight,' only to wake up in bed eight hours later, cradling a cold McDonald's and smelling like tequila. At the end of the day, it didn't matter what rules I laid out for myself, because I rarely ever stuck to them. This meant that I felt even worse the next day because I berated myself for not being able to drink like 'normal people' and concluded that I was, in fact, useless at everything.

The last thing I've learned that suggests drinking in moderation is not for me is that I am the type of person who doesn't even like (or rather, doesn't see the point in) two or three drinks. My whole motivation in drinking was to get drunk. Not just silly, giggling drunk, but wild and reckless drunk. That's not going to happen while moderating, so the two or three drinks might as well be alcohol-free.

Is Sobriety the Next Trend?

You'll have likely seen news coverage that reports sobriety is the next trend in wellness. This kind of declaration fills me with an equal sense of pride and horror that I can't quite put my finger on.

When I think of trends, I tend to think of things that come and go, almost before they've even arrived. Declaring sobriety to be a trend is a bit like saying feminism is a trend, because, quite honestly, it isn't. Sobriety is a rebellion. It's an awakening, an uprising. It's a lifestyle overhaul in the same way that veganism or sustainability is, and it's one that I genuinely believe is here to stay.

On the flip side, I do quite enjoy the fact that sobriety is being seen as 'trendy', because when I first went sober it felt far from it. Ultimately, something being trendy means perceptions about it change, the stigma attached to it drops, and people become a lot more accepting and open to the idea of it. From the off, my aim was to glamorize sobriety as much as we glamorize drinking; to fight fire with sparkly fire and show that being alcohol-free can be just as fun, cool and sexy as drinking.

Another advantage of sobriety becoming trendy is that bars are widening their non-alcoholic offering and their staff are becoming more receptive to non-drinkers' needs. Attitudes are changing to the point where some people have started to say that it's cool when I tell them I don't drink, rather than 'That's so boring.' Decreasing the stigma around sobriety can benefit all non-drinkers. The more people who embrace sobriety the easier it will be for all of us to recognize the benefits of avoiding alcohol altogether.

It is, of course, important to understand that there is a very serious side to giving up alcohol. For some people, getting sober isn't as easy as simply 'not drinking'. For these individuals, hearing sobriety being heralded as the next big trend is essentially putting it on the same level as bell-bottom jeans or Pokémon Go and somewhat diminishes their struggles. Acceptance of sobriety as a result of it being trendy can massively benefit those struggling with addiction and even those who have never drunk alcohol, but it's still important not to trivialize the issue by reducing this movement to flavoured tonics and morning dance parties.

Sober Girl Spotlight
'I started one of the first millennial sober blogs.'

Laurie McAllister (@laurievmcallister) stopped drinking when she was twenty-five, after she realized it was a contributing factor to her poor mental health during her early twenties.

> I started trying to stop drinking in 2015. I was living in London at the time, and every single person I knew drank. I'd been seriously struggling with anxiety and depression for about a year, and my blackouts and hangovers were getting worse. I spent a lot of hungover time at my desk, googling things like, 'Am I an alcoholic?' and 'Why am I having blackouts?'

Laurie started her blog, Girl & Tonic, on the same day she stopped drinking, and she is now over four years sober.

> When I was trying to quit, I found some US-based sober blogs, which really helped me, but they were all written by people quite a bit older than me. I felt really isolated, struggling with alcohol in my early twenties when all my friends seemed totally fine. On the day I decided my statement 'I am not drinking ever again' was going to stick, I started the

blog. I hoped it would help girls like me, who felt like they were the only ones struggling in a sea of people who appeared to be happily boozing it up. I said to myself that if it helps one person to feel less alone then I'll be happy.

Over the last few years, the conversation on sobriety has grown momentously. If you had told me when I decided to get sober that my life would be filled with wonderful sober friends and sobriety would (in some scenarios) be considered cool, I would never have believed you. It is so exciting to be able to attend brunches filled with sober women, and to read sobriety's health benefits being publicized in mainstream media. Deciding to stop drinking was hands-down the best thing I ever decided to do for my mental health (actually, my life in general). I am a better friend, have more money, and have the courage to follow my dreams. I am even writing this from my apartment in Cambodia.

Do I Need to Label Myself an Alcoholic?

The short answer to this is no. As far as I'm concerned, you don't need to label yourself as anything. In fact, the main reason I adopted the 'sober' label was because it seemed to give more weight to me turning down drinks at parties. I noticed that if I told people I didn't drink, they'd instantly want to know if I'd never drunk or if it was a new choice. Saying, 'I'm sober,' on the other hand, seemed to prompt fewer questions and made things a little bit easier at the beginning.

Over the last few years, there's been a lot of discussion around the words 'alcoholic' and 'alcoholism'. In fact, 'alcoholic' is now rarely used in medical literature, and is replaced by 'alcohol-use disorder', referring to the addictive nature of alcohol. Even the scientific thinking around alcoholism being an incurable illness is now widely contested. There is, after all, no official medical test that can diagnose you as an alcoholic – it is a decision left up to the drinker to decide upon for themselves.

A lot of us use the term without question, to designate that there are 'normal drinkers' and then there are alcoholics. You'll often hear people say things like, 'I'm drinking a lot, but it's not like I'm an alcoholic.' What we're hesitant to admit is that labelling other people is convenient for us all. For one, it allows us to keep drinking because we've adopted an 'us and them' narrative. In this version of events, we tell ourselves that normal people can keep drinking with no consequences, but alcoholics definitely can't. As long as we're not one, we can keep going.

This also means that a lot of us don't quit or cut down our alcohol consumption because we don't consider ourselves 'bad enough' to be one of them – the alcoholics. It means that a lot of us google and sigh with relief when we only meet some, but not all, of the criteria for a stereotypical drinking problem. We decide that we don't need to change our drinking habits, and we fail to acknowledge that alcohol can negatively impact our lives, even if we don't tick all the boxes on the questionnaire.

The stigma of these words can even hold people back from committing to sobriety, which was certainly true in my case. I was afraid that if I told people that I was sober, I would draw attention to the fact that I probably had a problem with drinking. I worried that behind my back people might whisper that I was an alcoholic, a label that – as a weekend binge-drinker – I didn't feel belonged to me, and thought might possibly be used against me. It felt like it would be slapped on me for life – that if I made the declaration, then there really was no turning back. Being the forward-planner and overthinker that I am, I even imagined my future children musing over the idea that their mother was an alcoholic, despite the fact she hadn't drunk for decades, and something about that just didn't sit right with me.

Strangely, a lot of us talk about the fact that alcoholism runs in the family, but according to Professor David Nutt, in his book *Drink? The New Science of Alcohol and Your Health*, you don't just inherit alcoholism. He states that 'In many cases you inherit one or more of the various different traits that make it more likely you'll be addicted, for example impulsivity or conduct disorder.'

This belief that alcoholism is only hereditary is another tick in the box for 'normal drinkers' – it means we think we'll probably be safe from the fate of alcoholism because our parents weren't addicted to it – when the truth is absolutely anyone can reach the level of alcohol dependency where your body becomes physically reliant on it.

When you think about it, it's really strange that alcohol is the only drug where we label the user this way. You are not a 'smoke-aholic', and even when you give up, you're an ex-smoker. When you pack in your nicotine habit, everyone cheers that you've conquered your addiction to the fags, but when it comes to society's view of alcohol, you're an addict for life. The problem is that words like 'alcoholic' and 'addict' can be stigmatizing. Using them can insinuate that the blame lies with the drinker, as if it is their fault that they can't handle the booze, and while I'm not suggesting we dodge all personal responsibility, the fact of the matter remains that alcohol is a dangerous and highly addictive substance that permeates every part of society. It is always around us, hard to escape from, and marketed to us so cleverly that being a drinker is the default and being a non-drinker is the deviation from the norm.

I won't tell you how (or whether) to label yourself – as we've already discussed, that is something only you can decide. We just need to recognize that these labels might be putting too much liability on the consumer and not enough on the toxically addictive product itself. Labels in general can empower us, but they can also keep us stuck.

Should I Go to Alcoholics Anonymous?

I'm often asked if I went to AA to get sober. The answer that you may or may not want to hear is no, I did not go to AA. There were two reasons behind my decision. The first was that I didn't want to call myself an alcoholic, for the explanations mentioned above, and the second was that I suffered from a very rare form of imposter syndrome, in which I genuinely believed that my drinking problem wasn't 'severe enough' for AA.

I believed that if I rolled up to a meeting and declared that I could quite easily go a week without drinking but still wanted help, I would be laughed out the room and told to come back when I had, at the very least, ruined all my relationships and maybe even lost my job.

The longer I've been running Sober Girl Society and the more sober women I've spoken to, the more I've heard and learned about AA. I've met some people who credit the fellowship with their sobriety and others who credit it with getting them sober but have since decided to stop attending meetings. I've met some people who have tried AA and hated it, and I've met people like me, who have years of sobriety under their belt having never set foot in a meeting.

It's my opinion that a person's relationship with sobriety can be incredibly complex, which is no surprise given we've all had different upbringings and reasons for drinking. I believe that what works for one person may not necessarily work for another, and I also believe that we should have the freedom to decide what works best for us.

A long time ago, AA was one of the only options for those who needed help with alcohol-related problems, and we are very lucky today that there are so many other choices. In recent years, AA has garnered a lot of criticism and been referred to as everything from 'cult-like' to 'patriarchal'. It is possible to get sober without its twelve-step programme – not just because I did, but because I have met hundreds of women who have done it too.

The main thing to note is that AA is free, and that is crucial, not to mention the millions of people who wouldn't be sober without it. There is the rationale that if you spend money on a sobriety course or a counsellor, you have more 'skin in the game' and are more likely to commit to something you've paid for, but it's important to remember that it's still very much a privilege to be able to afford help.

Lately, the conversation around AA has grown a little shouty, and in the online community there's an emerging divide between those who choose to go to AA and those who choose not to. So, in an effort to debunk some myths and have an honest chat around the subject, I consulted my friend Becky, who regularly attends AA meetings.

We met when she came to an SGS brunch – our sober anniversaries are only one week apart. Now thirty, Becky started drinking at thirteen, and by the time she stopped, she was experiencing an increasing number of blackouts and her behaviour during these blackouts was growing worse. She describes herself as a binge-drinker who was constantly waking up in places she didn't want to be, and spending her weekend outrageously hungover. In all honesty, her story sounds very similar to mine.

Becky had a friend who got sober through AA and she watched as this friend's life changed for the better. She was calmer and much happier, and Becky was also surprised because she wasn't the typical park-bench drunk she'd thought people who went to AA had to be.

After blacking out on a Tinder date, and with her friend's positive experience the convincer, Becky turned up to her first meeting. I asked if she had to sit in a circle, and she tackled my first misconception about AA by telling me that in most meetings there is definitely no circle! Her first meeting was a particularly small one, so she was immediately recognized as a newcomer, something I think would be terrifying for anyone with social anxiety, but she explained that people were just really keen to help her: 'They gave me their numbers and told me to ring them when I felt like picking up a drink, and told me about other meetings. I told them I wasn't a daily drinker and they said that drink problems have all sorts of different patterns.'

I asked Becky if this means I wouldn't have been laughed out of the room. She told me that a preamble is read out at the start of meetings which states that the only requirement for membership of AA is the desire to stop drinking.

For Becky, the first meeting wasn't a real turning point and nothing really changed. She had a second date lined up the following week and couldn't imagine going on it sober, so she drank instead and didn't go to another meeting for four months. By that point she had suffered another string of horrible blackouts. 'From then on, I started to attend regularly,' she explained. 'I enjoyed the meetings, but I didn't want to go more than once or twice a week, despite being told that as a newcomer I should try and come more often.'

Becky says she spent another four months with one foot in and the other out, until one day she woke up after a bender and something just clicked: 'I knew I didn't have to drink any more, for any reason. I often drank to drown out my anxiety, but for the first time I knew that the consequences of my drinking outweighed any motive to take the edge off.'

That's when Becky started engaging with AA properly and began to follow the twelve-step programme. She has been sober ever since and is clear proof that AA can work, even if you think that you're not enough of a problem drinker to be there. However, a lot of controversy still surrounds the process, so let's get stuck into the trickier aspects of the programme.

AA is well known for its religious dimensions (with a lot of mentions of the big guy in the sky), and for an atheist I imagine it would be quite hard to get on board. Becky told me, 'At my first meeting they said a prayer at the end and I remember thinking, "Well, I'll just have to ignore all this God stuff." What I came to realize, though, is that it isn't religious at all – but it is spiritual.'

She went on to say that a key part of the programme is the idea that she doesn't always have to be in control. In fact, when she finds herself being controlling (such as trying to change her partners and friends so that things turn out the way she wants them to), things usually go wrong, so the idea is to surrender the control to a higher power. Now she believes the more she surrenders to the flow of life and trusts that she is not running the show, the better things tend to work out for her. Becky explained that she has atheist friends in AA who follow the programme in their own way: 'Their idea of a higher power might be the love and positive energy within the room. I know someone else whose higher power is nature. Other people may have started out atheists but now have found some form of spirituality – I'd put myself in this bracket.' In this way Becky exposed misconception number two, which is that if you want to go sober you have to become God-fearing too.

Another major criticism of AA is the fact that it labels its members 'powerless'. A lot of people have picked up on the fact that women in particular already feel powerless, and perhaps those struggling with alcohol problems need to be built up rather than broken down. Becky explained how this might be taken out of context: 'The phrase refers to Step One of the programme, which is "We admitted we were powerless over alcohol – that our lives had become unmanageable."'

From her perspective this means admitting that we can't drink safely and that things have got out of hand. 'I do think that once I have a drink, I'm powerless over the outcome, or where it will take me. I don't think that takes away from my power as a woman, and the other women in AA have built me up and supported me throughout my sobriety.'

But what about the fact that AA seems to centre the blame on the individual and not necessarily the addictive substance that's been incredibly cleverly marketed to us? The literature of AA talks about defects of character and involves making a fearless moral inventory of ourselves. Becky said this is trickier to answer: 'I don't think that AA "blames" the drinker – it pretty much does the opposite, as alcoholism is viewed as an illness. But I do think that the programme and literature suggest that we have character defects such as fear and pride, which are unhelpful to us.'

According to Becky, she and some others she knows within the programme don't like to use the word 'defect' to describe these traits. If the literature had been written today, she thinks the terminology would be different. She supports the idea that alcohol is an addictive substance that is expertly marketed to us and she would like to see more awareness of this in meetings.

Taking into account everything you've just read about the word 'alcoholic', I asked Becky her thoughts on this and whether, as someone who attends AA, it's a label that she identifies with or not.

I do think the term alcoholic is problematic. I refer to myself as an alcoholic within AA – because I know that people there understand that it just means someone who's drinking in a problematic way. I don't ever refer to myself as one outside of AA though, because I don't think my drinking was much worse than many other binge-drinkers'. I also think that addiction is a spectrum and that many people have some level of dependence on alcohol.

I love the way Becky talks about AA and it clearly works for her, so I asked her why she feels the need to attend SGS meet-ups too.

> I go to AA to keep my ego in check, as often the discussions at meetings centre on thinking more than they do drinking, and to remind myself why I don't drink. I go to SGS meet-ups to find other girls around my age who still like to do fun things and drink mocktails and have a laugh. SGS has been so nice because it's brought other like-minded girls into my life. We can still go to a brunch and throw on a nice dress but there doesn't need to be any alcohol involved and I don't need to feel like the odd one out – the way I sometimes do when I'm surrounded by drinkers.

At that point in our conversation I wanted to cry because Becky had summed up exactly what I intended to do when I started SGS. I asked her if there was anything she'd like people to know about AA that would be important for this conversation. 'AA is by no means perfect,' she conceded, 'and sometimes I go through phases of barely going or feeling like it's a chore. You do get the odd pushy arsehole and people you don't like. But for the most part I try to follow the programme, and hang out with the people I like at the meetings I like, and I ditch the rest.'

To be honest, I'm not completely converted to the idea of AA, but I think that's more to do with the fact that I've come this far without it. Perhaps if I'd known Becky before I got sober I'd be more inclined to head on down to a meeting like she did, but nevertheless I'm so grateful for her honesty.

I love Becky's idea of taking the bits of AA that work for her and dumping the bits that don't, and the fact that she gets something unique from both AA and SGS meet-ups proves to me that sobriety isn't always this or that. I stand firm in my belief that humans are complex and need different things, but it reminds me that it doesn't need to be one thing or another – you can do a bit of everything if you wish. You can sample from the buffet of sober offerings and take what works for you from each. Ultimately, the choice is yours.

What Are My Other Options?

If AA isn't for you, or you count yourself on the more sober-curious side, then there are plenty of options for help with quitting or cutting down on your drinking. Instagram is awash with sober coaches, accountability groups and programmes, so help is never far away. Communities such as Club Soda have programmes dedicated to mindful drinkers, for those who want to cut down, take a break or quit, or you can join a sobriety school like Tempest if you're looking for something more permanent. Smart Recovery offers free in-person and online meetings, and their philosophy states that people are not their behaviours, so stigmatizing language, such as 'addict' and 'alcoholic', is not used.

One middle ground is to take part in the extended challenges that provide more support than your usual Dry January and Sober October. Alcohol Change UK's Sober Spring lasts for over ninety days, with regular email blasts and the chance to be in a group with other folk in your area, while One Year No Beer offers a 365-day challenge complete with daily videos and a five-week audio programme.

And then, of course, there is the Sober Girl Society! If you're already familiar with us then you'll hopefully know that SGS's social media and website is flooded with free content including resources, stories, tips and advice, not just from me but from sober women all over the world.

There is heaps of video content and booze-busting information as well as all the details about our meet-ups and events – which range from bottomless boozeless brunches to our Sober Sweat classes at Pineapple Dance School – and where, if you haven't already, you can meet like-minded women who are also changing, considering changing their relationship with alcohol, or have never drunk. For those who are new to us, you do not have to be full-time sober to come to one of our events, you just have to give not drinking a go throughout it.

When Is the Right Time to Give Up/Cut Down?

I get it: you can't give up this week because you've got that work thing, and then next week it's Leanne's thirtieth. The month after that you're going on Katie's hen do to Ibiza, so you couldn't possibly do it then, and after that it's Charlotte from work's wedding and we're kind of creeping into Christmas party season, but after *that*, maybe?

Believe me, I've heard every excuse for why now isn't the right time to give up or take a break from booze, and many of them have come out of my own mouth. The truth is there is never a good time to get your drinking in check. There will always be something to stop you, even if it's the glorious summer weather. The right time is now, before you talk yourself out of it, before you have time to over-think it, and while I give you the tools to do it.

Am I Too Young or Too Old to Stop Drinking?

I'm often on the receiving end of comments related to sobriety and my age – usually that I'm too young to give up drinking or that someone wishes they'd done it when they were my age (I was twenty-six when I stopped). It is categorically never too early or too late to make a positive change in your life. I don't care how ancient you think you are – you might live until you're one hundred – and I don't care if you're eighteen, because imagine how amazing your life will be if you never have a hangover to hold you back from living it to the full. The right age to give up drinking is when *you* feel that it's right – we're all on our own timelines and comparison is the thief of joy.

Am I Abnormal?

The short answer to this is no. Absolutely no one is supposed to be able to drink a vast amount of a toxic substance and feel absolutely fine for it, so if you view yourself as odd or weird, stop right there. You are certainly not abnormal and you are certainly not alone.

Being part of the Sober Girl Society shows me every day that I am not some kind of anomaly. There are quite literally thousands of us ladies out there who have realized that drinking is not for us, and I think that it's pretty incredible to be part of this community.

This includes sober celebrities too. In a way, I feel like we instantly have something in common, and should we ever meet we'll always have an in-joke to share about not drinking.

When I worry about things like attending big events such as a best mate's wedding sans booze, I often try to think about hordes of Hollywood A-listers attempting to navigate award ceremonies such as the Oscars while sober. I don't often feel sorry for the rich and famous, but I definitely feel relieved that I'll only have to navigate weddings with my friends' dodgy uncles while sober and not fancy bashes with some of the biggest names in showbiz.

Here follows an inspiring list of female stars flying the sober flag, to prove that even the glitziest and most glamorous who walk amongst us enjoy their Christmas without a glass of prosecco.*

♥ Adwoa Aboah
♥ Blake Lively
♥ Brené Brown
♥ Charlie Brooks
♥ Christina Perri
♥ Christina Ricci
♥ Daisy Lowe
♥ Davina McCall
♥ Davinia Taylor
♥ Demi Lovato
♥ Demi Moore
♥ Denise Welch
♥ Elle Macpherson
♥ Eva Mendes
♥ Florence Welch
♥ Gillian Jacobs
♥ Jada Pinkett Smith
♥ Jameela Jamil
♥ Jamie Lee Curtis
♥ Jane Lynch
♥ Jennifer Hudson
♥ Jennifer Lopez
♥ Jessica Simpson
♥ Kat Von D
♥ Kate Moss
♥ Kelly Osbourne

---

* Correct at time of publication.

- ♥ Kim Cattrall
- ♥ Kristin Davis
- ♥ Lala Kent
- ♥ Lana Del Rey
- ♥ Lena Dunham
- ♥ Leona Lewis
- ♥ Lily Allen
- ♥ Lisa Riley
- ♥ Lucy Hale
- ♥ Marian Keyes
- ♥ Meg Mathews
- ♥ Melanie Griffith
- ♥ Melanie Sykes
- ♥ Miley Cyrus
- ♥ Naomi Campbell
- ♥ Natalie Portman
- ♥ Ruby Rose
- ♥ Sadie Frost
- ♥ Sarah Millican
- ♥ Shakira
- ♥ Shania Twain
- ♥ Sia
- ♥ Stevie Nicks
- ♥ Tyra Banks
- ♥ Zendaya
- ♥ Zoe Ball
- ♥ Zoella

Hang On, Is Sobriety Part of Diet Culture?

In recent months there have been a few less than complimentary articles circulating the internet which liken sobriety to diet culture and declare that going sober is the new 'calorie counting', which let me tell you it most definitely is not.[3]

Why are the two so different? First, unlike food, you don't need alcohol to survive. Second, restricting calories and cutting out food groups is potentially very dangerous whereas cutting out or restricting alcohol is not. Unless you have an alcohol dependency (in which case your detox process should be done under medical supervision), there are zero health drawbacks when you remove alcohol from your life. In terms of your long-term mental and physical health it will only affect you in positive ways.

There is a very stark difference between constricting ourselves to be smaller and fit in versus liberating ourselves to be true and authentic. Sobriety is not a restriction: you take away one thing and you gain a shedload of other amazing things such as time, money and a new level of self-love. Dieting is about less but sobriety is about so much more.

When it comes to self-love, we've spent the last few years championing the acceptance of natural bodies and I think it's about time we did the same with our personalities. Rather than trying to make ourselves more fun, likeable and outgoing, using booze to bring out some kind of bravado, I wonder what would happen if we all started being a little more personality positive by accepting our perceived flaws and learning to love them. What would happen if we stopped caring whether people thought we were a bit awkward or a little boring?

Sobriety has allowed me to embrace my uptightness as a reminder that I can always be trusted in a crisis (because I always have a back-up plan), and my friends value having someone who organizes the secret Santa. Besides, there are plenty of other ways to let my hair down that don't involve me drinking copious amounts of wine.

We still have a lot to do in the area of self-love. However, I think it's important to keep in mind that taking alcohol out of the equation is really just another way of moving closer towards the naturally real and authentic you.

Does Sobriety Count as Self-care?

Absolutely! Your body is on a constant mission to protect you. Even when you're asleep, keeping you alive and healthy is a full-time job it doesn't even get paid for. Therefore, there's no better way to thank your body for looking after you than by saving it from the damage caused by alcohol. As you'll find out in the next chapter, it's potentially a lot.

Is My Life Going to Change?

Yes! If you're cutting down it will change a little, and if you're giving up it'll change a lot. But the good news is it'll only be for the better, and I and the Sober Girl Society will be there every step of the way.

PART TWO

Reaping the Rewards

3

Let's Get Fizzical

Alcohol and your body

The *Great Gatsby* author F. Scott Fitzgerald wrote that 'Too much of anything is bad but too much Champagne is just right.' The quotation is now so popular that you can buy it on a print to hang in your kitchen and reassure yourself that there is no such thing as too much Moët. That being said, it doesn't take much investigation to find out that Fitzgerald passed away at the ripe old age of forty-four from a heart attack thought to be associated with his excessive drinking. An article in *The Journal of the American Medical Association* states that 'Fitzgerald drank and smoked himself into a terminal spiral of cardiomyopathy, coronary artery disease, angina, dyspnoea, and syncopal spells.'[1] In Fitzgerald's case, too much champagne was a bad thing after all.

Though it might seem like an extreme case, this tale is a reminder that the stories we tell ourselves when it comes to booze and its health implications aren't always factually accurate, and there are some myths that need serious debunking.

Considering we are a nation of label-checkers with increasingly complex dietary requirements, it feels odd that we don't put alcohol under the microscope more. It is, after all, a toxic compound used as both a fuel and a solvent. More disturbingly, if it were discovered today, the safe limit once you've applied food standards criteria would be one glass of wine a year.[2]

Let's be honest, though – we all know that alcohol isn't great for us. I doubt there's anyone here who believes gin constitutes one of their five-a-day, or thinks that prosecco is on a par with kale as a superfood. But considering how much knowledge we have about the dangers of alcohol, we seem to be really reluctant to take the time to truly acknowledge the health risks. I don't want to spend this chapter using scare tactics to ensure you never drink again, but I do think it's important for everyone to know what the risks are in real terms, so that we can all make better and more informed choices in the future.

More than that, I want to show you there isn't a single part of your physical health that won't be improved by binning the booze. From the possibility of lengthier, luscious locks to a more robust immune system, saying no to wine o'clock is – in my opinion – the most effective, cheapest and most underrated health and beauty secret going, but more than that, ditching the drink might just save your life. Here's the best bit: you don't need to stock up on chia seeds, you don't need a juicer and there is no downloadable PDF plan. All you need to do is cut out one teeny-tiny thing (granted, it might not feel that way right now) and reap the overwhelming host of benefits outlined here.

Now, a quick disclaimer: at first, there's a chance that your skin might get worse when you stop drinking; there's a chance your hair might not instantly give Rapunzel's a run for its money;

and there's definitely a chance that you won't develop abdominal muscles overnight – and it's all OK. From talking to a lot of SGS girls, it seems that often things appear to get worse before they get better, and a lot of people claim to experience the outwardly physical benefits of sobriety further down the line.

Perhaps it's a shock to the system and your body needs time to adjust? I wish there was more science on this, but in the meantime you'll just have to believe me when I say that if none of these superficial changes happen for you immediately – or ever – it doesn't mean you're doing it wrong. We're all unique in our own bodies and likely to experience different results in response to new-found sobriety. At the end of the day it really doesn't matter if you look better, as long as you feel better, and even if your outsides don't show it your insides will be glowing.

First Things Female

If fighting the gender pay gap and constantly battling for rights over our own bodies wasn't exhausting enough, alcohol has a sexist agenda too. Thanks to us girls having a higher percentage of body fat and a lower percentage of water than men, we're generally at a greater risk of developing conditions that are a result of the negative impacts of alcohol, such as liver disease and heart damage, because it's more concentrated in our blood. Add to this the fact that alcohol can have an effect on our periods, our chances of conceiving and our menopause (is nothing sacred?) and we really do have a shittier deal.

Dreamy Sleep

Much like alcohol, sleep (or, specifically, a lack of it) can have a serious effect on your overall health. When you snooze, it is your body's chance to repair itself. Your cells regenerate, your brain flushes out toxins (though sadly not those thoughts of your ex) and your energy is restored. The thing is, dozing off under the influence of alcohol will never offer you a fully restful night's sleep, even though you might be fooled into thinking it will. While you might have no trouble nodding off initially, your sleep cycle gets massively disrupted after a few bevvies – particularly the REM (rapid eye movement) stage, which is important for mental health and overall wellbeing.

According to the National Institute of Neurological Disorders and Strokes, a study which involved depriving rats of REM sleep significantly shortened their life span – from two or three years to just five weeks.[3] While I appreciate you're not a rat, it's still vital research to show how important it really is to get in those quality zzzs.

Glowing Skin

If you're a babe who's obsessed with her cosmetics, then you'll know that even a casual scroll through any beauty retailer's skincare section will bring up a plethora of lotions and potions promising a tight, dewy, all-round radiant complexion. These pricey products promise to make you look as if you've either ingested the elixir of youth or been heavily photoshopped. In fact, you might not be surprised to learn that in 2017 UK women spent £1.5 billion on skincare. But you can, in fact, get all these benefits (and more) when you give up drinking, and it won't cost you a small fortune. Here are just a few reasons why alcohol isn't the best tonic for your skin.

Dark circles

As you know, alcohol is a buzzkill on your sleep, and if you don't get enough shut-eye, your blinker bags are sure to be much more prominent thanks to a decrease in cellular turnover. But more than this, alcohol causes the blood vessels in your skin to dilate, which makes dark circles even more obvious. And, as if alcohol didn't know not to kick you when you're already down, the dehydration it causes means that any discolouration under your eyes will become more prominent. A triple delight!

Redness and inflammation

When I used to drink, I looked like I was in a state of constant embarrassment, which to be fair, I probably was. My cheeks often felt red and hot, and I remember googling it and finding out that alcohol flush is a common side effect of drinking. Facial reddening is actually a sign that you might be a little bit intolerant to booze – the alcohol inflames tissue and this can create a reaction.

You might think this isn't a big deal, especially if it dissipates quickly the next day (which mine always did), but if you continue drinking in the same way, it could eventually persist and become a prominent and permanent facial redness.

Puffiness

I remember coming back from university one summer and my mum greeting me by telling me how my face had got rounder (mums have such a way with words!). After furiously stomping on the scales and finding out that I hadn't actually put on much weight, I concluded that maybe her eyeballs had got rounder.

Unfortunately, there is some science behind her assertion. Dehydration caused by alcohol (there's a theme here) causes your skin and vital organs to go into panic mode. They start clinging on to water for dear life, hence the bloated face.

Spots

You'd be forgiven for thinking that if your skin is drier then it will be less oily and therefore less spot-prone, but you'd be wrong. Alcohol dilates your pores, which offers the perfect environment for spots to flourish. A word to the wise from skincare expert Karen J. Gerrard:

When you first stop drinking, the toxins will be coming out your body through the skin, which can cause severe breakouts. Persevere, drink plenty of water to replenish moisture and get yourself into a good skincare routine. Cleanse, tone and moisturize twice a day, use a hydrating mask and exfoliate once a week – within a couple of weeks you will notice a difference.

Fine lines

You guessed it, dehydration is behind this one too. When it comes to drinking, we actually dehydrate from the inside out. Alcohol is a diuretic, meaning it makes your toilet trips more frequent and you therefore lose a lot more fluid. It also depletes your vitamin A reserves, which are essential for keeping your skin both firm and youthful. So bank your Botox money and bin the booze instead.

A Golden Glow

I remember reading in Catherine Gray's *The Unexpected Joy of Being Sober* that she believed that not drinking enabled her to tan better. When she researched it, she found that your body needs a shedload of vitamin B to get its bronze on, and alcohol is known for depleting our levels of it. I fully concur. Whether it's down to Catherine's vitamin-B theory or perhaps because I'm no longer up at the pool bar every five minutes, since going sober I tan better than I ever did before. Though to be clear, I'm still no golden goddess – more sun-kissed English rose.

Interestingly, on the flip side, some research shows that drinking alcohol can make you more likely to burn, which may have more to do with the fact that we become a lot less vigilant about sunscreen application after we've had a few drinks. Hence the slight scarring I have from when I horrifically burnt my chin in Ayia Napa in 2011.

Either way, sun safety should always be of paramount importance. Don't take this as advice to ditch the sunscreen now your bod is booze-free. Slap on that SPF like there's no tomorrow, whether you're sober or not!

An Instant Manicure

Although I don't reckon you could infer much from my pastel acrylics, it's generally thought that your nails are an indicator of your overall health because they need a constant supply of nutrients to grow well. As alcohol interferes with your uptake of nutrients through its effects on your digestive system and the absorption of vitamins and minerals, you could risk developing a vitamin deficiency. Unfortunately, because your nails aren't a vital organ, your body doesn't prioritize them when distributing nutrients and they can end up brittle, pale and peeling – sadly, not this season's talon trend.

A Better Barnet

Did I mention that alcohol dehydrates you? As a result, your hair can become dry and more likely to fall out. Anyone who knows me knows that I've coloured my hair since I was about fourteen, which means drinking, for me, was practically adding insult to injury. Now my mane is always in good condition, despite the bleach, and I've even sprouted some rogue new baby hair.

Brighter Eyes

When I stopped drinking, friends told me that they thought I had a new sparkle in my eyes. I assumed this was just one of those stock phrases people say (I also had a lot of 'You look more like you again'), but after a while I did start to notice that my eyes seemed a lot bluer and less bloodshot.

According to traditional Chinese medicine, every organ in the body is associated with a sense, and in the case of the liver, the meridian is thought to open into the eyes. So if you experience eye problems such as itchiness or dryness, for example, the theory is that the problem is perhaps not your eyes but your liver. By this logic, it could quite possibly be that because my liver is healthier my eyes are too.

A Nose for It

When you give up alcohol you will smell better. I don't mean that your body odour improves (though, truth be told, when you spend less time in nightclubs you will start to have a nicer whiff) but that your sense of smell will upgrade, as heavy drinking can impair it.

Weight Loss

As an advocate for self-love and body acceptance, conversations around weight loss and sobriety feel tricky to me. I believe that sobriety is one of the best things that you can do for your health, but I also know that BMI is *not* an accurate measure of health and therefore I'm always loath to talk about it. I've been asked in so many interviews whether I lost weight when I gave up drinking, and my standard response is always yes, I lost the weight of all my problems.

The way I try to have perspective is that any weight loss from quitting alcohol is only a side effect and should be seen as such — it's something only some people will experience and should never be a focus in and of itself. Some people lose weight when they stop drinking because they're no longer consuming thousands of calories from alcohol and trips to McDonald's at the end of a night; others may gain weight through comfort eating as they become accustomed to their new way of life (which is a perfectly reasonable coping mechanism); and many people remain exactly the same weight because our bodies are strange and unusual machines that will often strive to maintain homeostasis.

The other more serious health benefits of quitting drinking stated here make any effect it may have on your weight utterly inconsequential. Basically . . . who cares? You have bigger achievements advancing on the horizon now, so please don't be disheartened if you don't lose weight. If you follow anyone who has binned the booze on social media, you'll likely see a host of #TransformationTuesday posts showcasing everything from glowing skin to weight loss, but like I mentioned earlier, it doesn't work that way for everyone, so please keep that in mind.

Quitting booze will enrich your life in so many ways. Whatever size your sober body ends up being will be the least interesting thing about you.

Sober Girl Spotlight

'I have never felt healthier than I do in sobriety.'

Singer and songwriter Lucy Spraggan (@lspraggan) gave up drinking in 2019 after noticing the physical impact that alcohol was starting to have on her health: 'I was lazy, tired, constantly covered in mystery bruises, and even my vision seemed worse when I was hungover – though temporary, that's pretty scary.'

When she hit six months sober, Lucy started running: 'The first time I ran 2.4 km and vowed I would never do it again. Then I went the next day, and the next day after that. Three weeks later I did my first 10K. Now (unless I'm injured) I do at least four runs a week, including a weekly half marathon.' She says that she can now rely on herself to do the things she needs and wants to: 'Sobriety taught me the discipline I needed to live a more athletic lifestyle.'

Since ditching the drink, Lucy's physical health has been transformed in every way.

There are so many physical changes, it's almost hard to describe them all. Sobriety has even revealed that I'm lactose intolerant. I'd been putting various pains and issues down to hangovers or generally not feeling good through drinking. The whole thing has been a revelation. My body is worth so much more to me now.

Lucy says that for all the hard moments of sobriety, there are one hundred beautiful, breathtaking, liberating moments that will open up a world you didn't know existed: 'I know I sound like I'm part of a cult, that I feel like I'm "enlightened", but honestly, that is just my truth. Being sober is the best thing I've ever done.'

A Better Defence

When I was drinking, I was forever succumbing to colds, and for days after I'd been out I rarely ever felt the picture of health. Immunologist Dr Jenna Macciochi, author of *The Science of Staying Well,* told me that booze has a direct impact on our immune system, as well as affecting it indirectly through poor-quality sleep.

Drinking to excess can affect production of immune cells produced in the bone marrow and these are needed to replace older cells that are less effective. People who drink alcohol excessively also tend to be at an increased risk for infectious diseases, take longer to recover from illnesses and have more complications after surgery.

She also notes that heavy alcohol intake can affect organs that regulate immunity, such as the liver, which produces proteins that ward off bacterial infections, and it can impact immunity through our gut too.

Excess alcohol can also damage the lining of the gut, where 70 per cent of the body's immune system is located. Those who drink regularly are more likely to suffer from gut dysbiosis (an imbalance of gut bacteria).

Symptoms of this can include bad breath, diarrhoea, and vaginal or rectal itching – so you know for sure it's something you don't want to end up with. Dr Macciochi points out that gut dysbiosis is more common in individuals who drink spirits, such as gin, because these drinks decrease the number of beneficial gut bacteria. Something to think about when you're next tempted by that G & T!

Here's another fun fact: immune cells in the brain are responsible for the clumsiness we associate with alcohol. Dr Macciochi says that from the research it appears that both a binge-drinking dose and a lower moderate dose of alcohol rapidly activate special immune cells in the brain. They produce pro-inflammatory signalling molecules, which appear to be critical to alcohol-induced sedation and motor impairment by influencing how our nerve cells work.

More Energy

I'm going to run the risk of sounding super smug here, but since embracing sobriety I have become a morning person. The reason I feel so smug about this fact is that for twenty-six years I was the complete opposite. In fact, it was rare for me to ever see the morning on a weekend because waking up at 2 p.m. was not uncommon.

Essentially, as well as giving you a less than satisfactory night's sleep, alcohol also interferes with the way your body produces energy. Because your liver loves you, it works hard to frantically break down the booze in your system in order to keep you safe and ensure that you remain relatively unpoisoned. This means that producing glucose ends up further down its to-do list and results in lower levels of blood sugar, which might be the reason behind your fatigue.

A Smoother Cycle

I'm definitely more in tune with my own body now that I'm sober, especially when it comes to my time of the month. I'm now able to tell with exact precision when I'm about to come on my period, regardless of whether I mark it on my calendar or not.

There's one day just before the red river floweth when I am so ravenous I could eat everything, and another when I'm so easily irked that I demonstrate frustration at everything – and, more specifically, everyone. Now that I know none of these irritations are down to a hangover or the impacts of alcohol on my hormones and mental state, I'm so much more in touch with Mother Nature and my own needs. It means I'm able to manage both days much better, which for me equates to wearing anything with an elasticated waist and avoiding all human contact.

Apart from my new-found clarity when it comes to my hormones, it's important to know that women who drink excessive amounts of alcohol can experience menstrual disorders including amenorrhea (an absence of a period for three or more months), irregular cycle lengths and anovulation (an absence of ovulation in a cycle). Despite the pain and discomfort periods can cause, it's essential to recognize they are vital and necessary to reproductive health. I'm lucky to have a regular cycle, and I'm so glad that it isn't something I'm taking for granted any more.

A Baby Boost

As I am yet to attempt to bear a child, I am turning purely to established science for this one. Researchers from Harvard University found that drinking more than six units a week (which is about three small glasses of wine) can reduce a woman's chance of conceiving by 18 per cent.[4] This is why some doctors recommend that you quit drinking if you're trying to get pregnant, and especially if you're going through IVF. Whether you see it as good or bad, it's worth bearing in mind that you might be more fertile than usual when sober.

Despite the fact that a lot of my mum's friends were told to drink a daily pint of Guinness for iron, there is only one party line on alcohol intake during pregnancy these days, and it's a very clear guideline that *no* amount is safe to consume when you're carrying. Drinking in the first three months of pregnancy can increase the risk of miscarriage and premature birth. Drinking after the first three months can affect your baby's health once they are born, with the risks including them having learning difficulties and behavioural problems. Drinking heavily throughout pregnancy can cause your baby to develop foetal alcohol syndrome, for which there is no treatment.[5]

We all have a part to play in this of course, which is supporting our expecting friends in not drinking. Nine months of continuous sobriety can be hard, and a part of the whole pregnancy process that is not often acknowledged. Recognizing the achievement and not encouraging someone to 'have a glass of champers' at their baby shower are important.

Decreased Cancer Risk

See how I eased you in with the benefits to your skin and nails, and now I'm going to hit you with the hard stuff? Sneaky, I know.

In 1988, alcoholic beverages were declared carcinogenic, but only in 2020 did the American Cancer Society update its guidance to stipulate that it is best to avoid alcohol completely. The previous advice was for women to limit their intake to one drink a day, and for men to drink only two. While ethanol is thought to be the major problem (due to the fact it is known to increase the cancer risk at even moderate drinking levels), alcoholic drinks are more complex than we think and may contain other known carcinogens, such as lead and formaldehyde.

This is what we know – alcohol has links with seven different types of cancer: bowel, breast, laryngeal (voice box), liver, mouth, oesophageal (food pipe) and pharyngeal (upper throat). The scary truth is that for some of these cancers, your risk of developing them increases with even moderate drinking. For example, just a single drink a day can increase your risk of breast cancer and this statistic is the reason I started Booze-free Boobs – a campaign to highlight the dangers of alcohol and its link to breast cancer.

I think it's important to point out that when it comes to the big

C, neither the type nor the price of the alcohol matters. Cancer doesn't care if you're drinking Red Stripe from a can or Dom Pérignon from a crystal flute. You cannot cheat or buy your way out of the disease. One thing for sure is that we spend a lot of time fundraising for charities such as Cancer Research UK, and this is the research they have provided.[6] You have the information, so until we find a cure for cancer, sobriety is one very clear way to minimize your risk.

A Better Brain

The short-term effects of alcohol on the brain can include blurred vision, slurred speech and difficulty walking: all things that we accept as common signs that someone has had a bit too much of the sauce.

Over time, other effects of alcohol become scarier and more extreme – in the long term, even moderate drinking can cause brain damage. Your brain cells can start to change and get smaller, and too much booze actually shrinks your brain, affecting how you think, learn and remember things.[7] It's thought that women may experience brain damage at lower levels of alcohol intake than men.

According to Professor David Nutt, at least one in five cases of dementia is probably the result of long-term alcohol consumption, and an extensive thirty-year study found evidence of faster cognitive decline in people who drank up to seven units each week (two large glasses of wine is six units) than in teetotallers – showing that even moderate drinking may damage the brain.[8]

Healthier Liver

When we talk about the negative impacts of alcohol, you'll often hear your liver mentioned because it is the main organ that processes alcohol and removes toxins from the bloodstream. Essentially, it's your body's personal bouncer.

If you drink too much, fat will start to build up in your liver (known as hepatic steatosis) and this fat starts to damage the cells around it. If you take a break from alcohol, your liver can start to repair itself, but if you keep drinking too much you will scar the liver permanently. This is known as liver cirrhosis, a very serious condition which is irreversible and symptoms of which include vomiting blood, yellow skin, permanently swollen legs, and a bulging stomach from a build-up of fluid.

At this point I'm hoping you'll have realized why dewy skin and a smaller waist aren't necessarily the best body benefits you might experience from breaking up with booze, and that the most important changes are the ones you can't even see.

Stronger Heart

Strong girls need strong hearts and sadly booze doesn't help with that. Not only does drinking weaken the heart muscle, rendering it less efficient and less powerful at pumping blood, but alcohol poisons your heart in the same way it poisons your liver, which can eventually lead to heart failure.

Even light-to-moderate drinking can raise your risk of developing an irregular heartbeat, and alcohol is the leading preventable cause of hypertension (increased blood pressure), which can be extremely dangerous as it can result in heart attacks and strokes.[9]

It Might Just Save Your Life

If I had a pound for every time I've fallen over drunk or woken up with mysterious scrapes after a night out, I would be a very rich woman. While I am delighted that I no longer have the bruised legs of a six-year-old who's been running around in the playground, it's important to note that drunken injuries can be life-altering – and even life-ending – for some.

Alcohol misuse is the biggest risk factor for death, ill health and disability among 15–49-year-olds in the UK, and in Scotland 15 per cent of all deaths in young people aged 16–24 are linked to alcohol.[10]

There are horrific cases of tragic accidents that occurred as result of drinking, and recent stories in the news include a thirty-three-year-old young mother who died after falling down a flight of stairs and cracking her head open; a crew member who died after breaking her spine when she fell down the steps to her cabin on the boat she was staying on; and the student who was crushed to death after drunkenly falling asleep in a bin.[11]

As well as accidents, drinking too much can also lead to alcohol poisoning, and over the years there have been many notable student deaths which have sparked concerns about university drinking culture. I probably wouldn't have started drinking as much as I did without university, and can safely say that the way alcohol is tied up in the culture of higher education needs to change. Alcohol poisoning most commonly happens when you consume a lot of alcohol in a short period of time (what we commonly refer to as a 'binge'), and some of the inquests into these accidents have cited the initiation rituals that can take place amongst students during Freshers' Week and at sports team socials.

Last but not least, there is the huge matter of alcohol being an addictive substance. Despite the fact that it can cause us so much pain, drinking can also give us pleasure; it floods our brains with endorphins and because of this rush, we want more. But the more we drink, the more our tolerance to it builds, so over time we need greater amounts of alcohol to reach the same level of intoxication.

There are a lot of complex factors and a lot of unanswered questions around addiction, such as what role our genes play and whether there is such a thing as an addictive personality. There are whole books on the subject, so if you're interested in diving deep into the neuroscience, I've provided details in the support and resources section (see pages 279–289) of the best ones to look at.

But Wait a Minute, Isn't Red Wine Good for You?

When you give up drinking, people will likely say things like 'Red wine has antioxidants in it.' My standard comeback is to state that blueberries have antioxidants in them too, but I've never thrown up in my handbag or slept with a stranger after eating them. If you need something more concrete to go on, then write this down on a piece of paper and keep it handy:

♥ In 2018, a large global study published in *The Lancet* (a leading medical journal) confirmed previous research that has shown there is no safe level of alcohol consumption. The researchers admit moderate drinking may offer some level of protection against heart disease by boosting levels of good cholesterol in the blood, but found that the risk of cancer and other diseases outweighs these protections.[12]

So even if red wine is good for your heart, it's still not good for you overall, which I understand is confusing given how many articles scream from the rooftops about why you should be drinking it.

Protecting Our National Health Service

I adore the NHS. I think the UK is quite possibly the luckiest country in the world to have such an incredible group of people looking after us. But it's no secret that the NHS is grossly over-stretched and incredibly underfunded, something that isn't helped in any way by the nation's drinking.

In England alone, during 2018–19, there were 1.26 million hospital admissions related to alcohol consumption. This equates to 7.4 per cent of *all* hospital admissions, and that figure is 8 per cent higher than the previous year. This means that there are approximately 3,452 alcohol-related admissions *every single day* – and that's without including statistics from Wales, Scotland or Northern Ireland.[13]

Not only that, but up to half of all people in beds on orthopaedic wards are there because of alcohol-related injuries,[14] and recent estimates have suggested that in the UK, three in four patients attending A&E at the weekend are there because of alcohol.[15]

All of this combines to show how alcohol-related problems cost the NHS £3.5 billion every single year. If you think that doesn't have anything to do with you because you only drink every now and then, you're wrong. It includes everyone from my friend's neighbour, who fell over in her garden when she was clapping for the NHS sozzled, to my brother's intoxicated pal who had to go to A&E when he drunkenly decided to put a lightbulb in his mouth and it got stuck. It includes even light-to-moderate drinkers who are still increasing their risks of developing an alcohol-related illness, and therefore the likelihood of needing NHS care in the future.

By not drinking, you are doing something incredibly important, not just for yourself and your health but also for the NHS and the people who need it. Sobriety is something that benefits you and can contribute towards a healthier, happier life for others too.

Sober Girl Gains

☐ A bouncier brain and bouffant

☐ Less chance of the seasonal sniffles

☐ A liver that loves you back

☐ A strong heart (which every strong girl needs!)

☐ A lot more blueberries!

4

Sobriety Over Hangxiety

Alcohol and your mind

B y the end of my drinking escapades it was quite obvious how much of an effect alcohol was having on my mental health. When people ask my mum about why I founded the Sober Girl Society, she explains it by saying, 'Booze really ruined her head.'

Having experienced first hand the transformative effect cutting out alcohol can have on your mind, I am frequently surprised that it rarely gets a mention when topics such as self-care and looking after your emotional wellness are brought up on social media or during television segments. Instead, we're normally advised to take deep breaths, increase our bubble-bath quota or start a gratitude journal. I'm not denying that these things can fortify your mental health, but I would gladly rank sobriety above them all in terms of effectiveness. (Plus, it's worth noting that bubble baths are normally sold to us with the image of a woman, wine glass in hand. Anyone who has attempted to balance a glass of Rioja in the tub will know that it is never as straightforward as it's made to look in photos.)

I've also been stunned by the recent surge in panel discussions and events in the mental health space that have tried to lure guests with the promise of swanky cocktails. I'd suggest that if you are already struggling with your mental health, alcohol is highly unlikely to contribute to it in a positive way – for lots of reasons, which I'll explain now. Buckle up.

Can Alcohol Really Impact Your Mental Health?

For a long time, the health warnings surrounding alcohol generally concentrated on our physical health (increased risk of cancer, heart disease, and so on), but in recent years the focus has shifted increasingly to the impacts on our mental health. In fact, in November 2020, the theme of Alcohol Awareness Week in the UK was 'alcohol and mental health'.

Drinking has been linked to a range of mental health conditions, such as depression and anxiety, and an increase in dialogue around this subject over the past few years has also meant an increase in research. One 2019 study, published in the *Canadian Medical Association Journal*, showed that lifetime alcohol abstainers report the highest level of mental wellbeing, and quitting alcohol improves mental wellbeing among women.[1]

Dr Michael Ni, co-author of the study, even explained that these findings suggested 'caution in recommendations that moderate drinking could improve health-related quality of life. Instead, quitting drinking may be associated with a more favourable change in mental wellbeing, approaching the level of lifetime abstainers.'

It's not looking good for binge-drinking – my former speciality – in particular, because a 2019 study in Singapore concluded that bingeing was found to be associated with myriad mental health conditions, including anxiety, and binge-drinkers reported a poorer quality of life compared to their non-bingeing counterparts.[2]

Unfortunately, alcohol and mental health is a very complex relationship because sometimes it's hard to establish cause and effect. Dr Gemma Newman (also known as @plantpowerdoctor on Instagram because of her specialist interest in holistic health and plant-based nutrition) has worked in medicine for sixteen years. She explains:

> A hangover can also be thought of as a mini-withdrawal from alcohol, and anxiety can be one of the components of this too. But many people who have issues with low mood or anxiety can use alcohol as a way to separate from the pain of these feelings. This makes the link between using alcohol for this purpose and feeling worse because of alcohol use, an intertwined phenomenon.

When I look back on my own history of mental health issues, it really is hard to tell what came first. I don't remember being a very anxious or depressed teenager, and really, my mental health issues only started at university – the same time that my drinking did. It could be that the natural stresses of adulthood gradually made me more anxious and a bit teary, so I drank more to cope. Or perhaps drinking really did cause my anxiety and feelings of depression in the first place. Either way, I found myself quickly caught in a cycle of trying to quieten my mind with booze, making things ten times worse, and then doing it all over again.

To arm you with some of the information we do have, I'm going to take you on a deeper dive into why booze could be causing your blues, and I'll endeavour to answer the age-old question – why, on a hangover, do I feel like all my friends hate me and I'm the worst human who ever lived?

Direct Effects

There are a couple of major ways in which alcohol can affect your mental health, and the first is, unsurprisingly, via your brain. Much like the rest of your body, your brain is finely tuned to keep you alive by managing some very delicate chemical processes, and when you drink you alter some of them. While some cognitive processes are stimulated when you booze, others are blocked or dampened, so it basically becomes complete chaos up there.

Even after you've stopped drinking, your brain carries on trying to put things right. Essentially, it's clearing up the absolute mess from the house party you've just had in your body. This is why you might feel a little 'all over the place' for a while after a heavy drinking session – your brain is performing a sort of frantic clear-up to set things back the way they were.

The second and lesser-known way in which alcohol can affect your mental health is via your gut. As discovered in the last chapter, alcohol is no good for your immune system, and a poorly one can contribute to inflammation in the body, which is associated with numerous mental health disorders, such as depression. Alcohol also stops you from absorbing some of the good stuff, such as vitamins and minerals, which you need for good mental wellbeing.

Indirect Effects

As well as minor things like changing your entire brain chemistry and inflaming your body, there are indirect ways in which alcohol (and hangovers) can affect your mental health. While there's no exact science behind this, here are a few things that I believe contributed negatively to my mental wellbeing when I was drinking:

- Never having any energy because of alcohol and therefore feeling lethargic and useless

- Not getting a good night's sleep, which is absolutely key for good mental health

- Never doing any exercise and getting those extra endorphins

- Always panicking because I had blacked out and couldn't remember things

- Feeling shameful about things I did while drinking

- Hardly getting outside or seeing much daylight on days when I had a hangover

- Feeling anxious that I'd said or done something silly while drinking

- Being paranoid that everyone hated me because of my drinking

- Always worrying about the money I'd spent

- Smoking, because drinking made me want to (and smoking is also shown to increase anxiety)

- Essentially living in squalor because I was too hungover to clean or tidy

- Barely touching a vegetable on a hangover

- Hating the way I looked (grey) because I wasn't taking care of myself

- Never spending my holidays relaxing, just being drunk or hungover

- Feeling guilty about wasting my weekend

- Wasting my weekend and not having a chance to relax before another week at work

- Cancelling plans and avoiding social connection on a hangover, which caused me to withdraw

Actually, after writing this list, I feel a bit embarrassed about the fact that I didn't realize sooner that alcohol was probably behind a lot of my mental health problems.

Blackouts

Have you ever woken up after a drinking session with zero recollection of events from the night before? Have you ever been told about something embarrassing that you did and you've been, like, 'OMG no, that definitely wasn't me' (when it definitely was)?

Have you ever felt like you're in a film where there's a club scene, and then the camera cuts and the next thing you know you've woken up in bed?

If the answer to any of these questions is yes, then you've probably experienced a blackout. While blackouts are clearly a very physical effect of alcohol, I often think that they had more of a negative impact on my mental health, which is why I've chosen to include them in this chapter.

The first thing to understand is that not everyone who has ever drunk has had a blackout. For a long time I thought it was totally normal to go out and not remember how I got home but alas, it is most definitely not. That said, they can happen to anyone.

So what's the science behind them? According to Dr Gemma Newman, 'An alcoholic blackout is amnesia for the events of any part of a drinking episode without an actual loss of consciousness. This means your memory of a night out is impaired, but you look to everyone around you as though you are aware of what you are doing. It's a dangerous and scary thing.'

Dr Newman says that some scientists have hypothesized there may be an element of selective memory attached to feelings of denial or guilt – especially when something happens during this 'lost time' which you feel embarrassed or ashamed about – but there are also specific pathways in the brain that alcohol impacts, which explains this phenomenon.

She also says that blackouts are associated with the speed at which your blood alcohol level goes up:

Normally, if someone drinks slowly, the brain begins adjusting to the alcohol to minimize its effects on brain function, whereas if someone drinks quickly, the memory circuits have no time to adjust and can get shut down. Memory circuits do not become tolerant of alcohol, so even if you are a heavy drinker, you can still walk around and black out without realizing.

According to Dr Newman, alcohol doesn't affect every part of the brain equally, but the limbic system (which is believed to process memories) seems particularly vulnerable to the anaesthetizing effects of alcohol: 'Because the process of encoding short-term memories into long-term ones is impaired, there is either partial (fragmentary) or complete (en-bloc) blackout potential.'

So, it turns out that you haven't forgotten what happened last night, but rather your limbic system didn't let you store those memories in the first place. Your memory of the night was literally not captured by your brain so that's why, try as you might, you may never remember why you bought five tequila shots and then proceeded to take your top off.

The part where it gets really weird is that while you're in a blackout, no one around you can really tell. You could be behaving perfectly normally, you could be dancing, chatting, even having sex, and yet you might not remember any of it. Some people have driven cars during a blackout, and even had road accidents, without any recollection of either. There have been some seriously scary stories that you can google if you really want to be kept up at night. *The Girl on the Train* by Paula Hawkins, where the main character cannot remember whether she has committed murder, is one of the better-known fictional depictions of how terrifying blackouts can really be.

I have experienced many a blackout, during which I have

done things that I still to this day have no recollection of. When it comes to sex and the issue of consent, it's a dangerous grey area – something we'll discuss in a little more detail later on.

It's worth mentioning again that while there are a lot of unknowns when it comes to blackouts, generally speaking, females are more susceptible to the effects of alcohol because of our slightly lower muscle- and body-mass, which increases the blood/alcohol volume at a faster rate. Dr Newman also points out that the amount of alcohol needed to produce blackouts impairs our balance, coordination, decision-making and impulse control, which can lead to unfortunate choices, injury and even death.

Blackouts are so unsettling that if you're not sure if you've ever had one, you probably haven't. When you know, you know. But just in case there is any confusion, allow me to walk you through my typical post-blackout morning.

At about 6 a.m. I'd usually wake up short of breath, like someone who has just resurfaced in the swimming pool after struggling for air. I'd frantically look around and prepare to jump into my role as Detective Inspector Millie. I would immediately call my friends (with no regard for the fact they might still be asleep) and attempt to interview them as if they were witnesses to a crime: Who had I been with? What did I say? What time did I leave? Are you pissed off with me?

Once I'd gathered this intel, the next stage would be to assemble and inspect the physical evidence, which ranged from decoding my receipts, scanning my call log and checking my body for any obvious signs of bruising before examining my Uber account to try to piece together my journey home. If this all sounds familiar, it's likely that you've experienced a blackout too.

As there isn't a lot of research around blackouts and mental health, I asked my followers some questions around the subject instead.

I was shocked to find out that out of the 924 people who answered my yes/no poll, 832 said that they had experienced a blackout. I actually noticed that a couple of my close friends answered no, which means that all the times I'd told them that I couldn't remember my night, they probably thought I was faking it because I didn't want to own up to all the ridiculous shit I'd done.

When it came to the duration of a typical blackout, the answers varied. Lots of people said 2–3 hours but there were plenty of people, like me, who admitted they'd lost entire nights to alcohol.

When I first started blacking out, I would lose a sporadic few hours of my night, but by the end of my drinking I barely remembered anything. Dr Newman says that while a single blackout might not tell us much about a person other than they drank enough to shut down their memory areas at least once, as the number of blackouts goes up, so do the odds of having an alcohol-use disorder. 'Blackouts can be scary,' she says, 'and most people who have experienced one will naturally reduce their drinking. If someone does not, it can indicate an issue of alcohol reliance because the positive associations of drinking outweigh the potential harms for them.'

When I asked my followers whether their blackouts had grown worse, the answers were completely mixed. Some people said absolutely yes, while others said they thought that they had improved along with their tolerance. Some said that their blackouts had been bad from day one, and one person even noted that they didn't really know what it was like to be drunk because they constantly blacked out. I definitely started to feel this way at the end of my relationship with alcohol: my friends used to remark how one minute I seemed stone-cold sober and the next minute they were picking me up off the floor. I rarely felt drunk in the months before I went sober – just completely with it or in complete darkness.

Like a lot of cold cases, I'll never solve some of the mysteries of my drinking, but I know I did plenty of things that I'm not proud of. As Amy Schumer says, 'Nothing good ever happens in a blackout. I've never woken up and been, like, "What is this Pilates mat doing out?"'

Eventually, blackouts really started to take a toll on my mental health. The unknown and blank spaces in my memory started to dominate my thinking time, and I became pretty paranoid too. I hated getting on trains or going back to certain bars because I wondered if the staff remembered me. I constantly felt ashamed and guilty for putting myself in those drunken situations, and not being able to remember things began to terrify me – to the point where on certain hangovers, I genuinely felt like I had lost my mind.

For a long time I thought I was alone in this: none of my friends seemed to have to spend their morning texting Uber drivers or reading nonsensical messages they'd sent to people they hadn't spoken to in years. But hallelujah, I have found my people, and here are a few musings from my followers who told me why blackouts *definitely* did affect their mental health.

> 'They give you major anxiety the next day.'
>
> 'They amplify feelings of shame, anxiety and lack of control.'
>
> 'They make you feel like another person.'
>
> 'They feel so embarrassing, not to know what happened.'
>
> 'They make you feel angry at yourself.'

'They are so draining and disappointing to deal with.'

'They create massive fear that you have been, or could have been, taken advantage of.'

'They make you not trust yourself.'

'They leave you thick with self-hatred.'

Reading these answers made me feel so sad. It also made me realize that I'd massively taken for granted how something as simple as remembering my own life could be so fundamental to my happiness. It's hard not to wonder how much blacking out, week in, week out, could be having serious consequences for the state of our minds, especially when it comes to those feelings of shame and self-hatred, which don't just disappear overnight.

Now, if only there was a word for that all-encompassing feeling of dread you experience after a night on the sauce . . .

Hangover Anxiety

The feeling of anxiety/fear/impending doom on a hangover is common. So common, in fact, that it has been given many 'affectionate' nicknames across the world. In the UK it's most commonly known as 'hangxiety', 'beer fear' or 'the Sunday scaries'; in Australia it's 'boozanoia'; and in Finland it's '*morkkis*', meaning 'moral hangover'.

Hangover anxiety, as we've discussed, can absolutely be a result of blackouts and memory lapses (wondering whether you snogged your friend's brother or accidentally called your boss a dick), but you might find that you can still feel a little on edge even if you do remember your entire night. Here's the science behind it, according to Dr Newman:

> The first thing to say is that people who tend to feel anxious may also tend to use alcohol to aim to limit or avoid these feelings. When your dopamine neurons start firing, this can feel good, but the action of other neurotransmitters like serotonin are also potentially interrupted. This can lead to all sorts of emotions – not just anxiety, but also low mood, impulsivity, agitation and irritability. When it comes to anxiety, the GABA pathway seems most important. GABA is an inhibitory neurotransmitter which is involved with movement control, memory and anxiety. Initially, its activation can make you feel fuzzy, calm or relaxed, but over time the opposite can occur, and the feelings you were trying to quell or avoid often return with a vengeance.

So, truth be told, alcohol doesn't ever fix your anxiety, it kind of puts a plug in it and then *realllly* lets you have it in the morning.

The science might be simple, but hangover anxiety is far from a walk in the park, especially when you combine missing memories and chemicals misfiring left, right and centre. I probed my followers on this one too, and asked what hangover anxiety felt like to them. Hundreds of responses hit the nail on the head:

> *'It's like you're constantly questioning yourself.'*
>
> *'It's a feeling of distress and not being able to cope with how you're feeling.'*
>
> *'It's pure panic.'*

'It's a tidal wave of all your fears and worries – all your
    dreads spring to the surface and erupt.'

'It's miserable, like a black hole.'

'It's an unwavering feeling of dread and sadness.'

'It's an apocalyptic doom of self-hate.'

'It gets so bad that I can't answer texts or calls and I'm
    too anxious to drive.'

'It's a horrible, heavy dread and a shame-like feeling in my
    chest.'

'It's utter self-hatred, replaying everything I said or did in
    the worst light possible.'

'It's emotional nausea.'

'It's having a bleak outlook on life in general.'

'It's like you've got a festering hole in your chest that is
    raw, painful and won't heal.'

'It's feeling like you are/everything is rubbish.'

'It's lingering uneasiness for a few days.'

'It's a crippling pain of fear that takes over your body.'

'It's being in your own worst nightmare.'

'It's an internal tornado.'

'It's a self-inflicted torture.'

'It's a full existential crisis – every time.'

If I had to provide a brief description of my own hangover anxiety, it was half 'feeling like I was the worst human who ever
lived, and my existence on the planet was pointless at best' and

half 'sheer paranoia about anything and everything'. Not only did I frequently google 'drunk girl London' because I became convinced that there was a viral video of me circulating on the internet, but I also became obsessed with the idea that I was both mentally and physically ill. On quite a few of my hangovers I managed to convince myself that I had cancer or schizophrenia. Generally speaking, I'd say I have minor health anxiety, but hangovers exacerbated it tenfold.

As well as clear mental symptoms of hangxiety, lots of people told me about their physical ones too, such as a pounding heart, restlessness, insomnia, shakes, a tight chest, feeling faint, shivers, shortness of breath, sweating, nausea, loss of appetite, upset stomach and, as two people put it, 'my bowels go fucking haywire' and 'the shits'. To be honest, it's no wonder I convinced myself I was dying.

When I asked my followers how long hangover anxiety lasted for them, the answers were again pretty varied. At the tamer end of the scale people said a few hours, and at the other end, over a week. The average was about 2–4 days. Personally, I would have said it was around three days before I felt back to normal(ish), so that sounds about right to me.

For those who are now sans booze, I also asked how much of a factor hangover anxiety was in their decision to go sober. Interestingly, hardly anyone said less than 50 per cent. In fact, most answers were around the 80–90 per cent mark, with tons of people adding that it was their absolute number-one reason for ditching drinking.

Why Now?

Over the last few years, several articles have appeared claiming there's been an uptick in those opting for teetotalism. *Elle Australia* examined 'The Rise of the Sober Curious Lifestyle' and asked the question 'Are we over alcohol?' But if so many of us are citing hangover anxiety as a reason for not drinking, it begs the question has it not always been a thing?

One of my theories is based on the increased self-awareness and kind of 'collective awakening' that we seem to be experiencing in the world. More than ever we are questioning things that we have always just taken as 'givens'. We're starting to ask whether things are actually making us feel good or if we're just doing them because everyone else is. We're making more conscious decisions about all aspects of our life, and that includes drinking.

My second major theory is that there are a lot of new layers to hangover anxiety. Social media means that every drunken move you make is now documented. Twenty years ago, you needn't have worried about snogging Barry from IT, but now you need to wake up and stress about the fact that Susan from Accounts has already uploaded a video to Instagram of you eating his face off. Similarly, even five years ago you could go to Ascot and merrily have a knees-up, whereas now it's probably only a matter of time before you spot yourself on the 'sidebar of shame', flashing your knickers after a bottle of rosé.

Social media also means we have a window into everyone else's world when we're hungover, and there's probably nothing that makes you question your relationship with alcohol more than seeing that Lucy from your old job has already baked spelt muffins and upcycled a chair before 10 a.m., while you're still trying to piece together what happened after you left the kebab shop.

Longer-lasting Damage

In 2019, I was interviewed for a *Telegraph* piece titled 'Can Giving Up Alcohol Improve Your Mental Health?' It was based around the new research from the Canadian study mentioned earlier but it also included a quote from Priory psychotherapist Peter Klein which, when I read it, summarized what I had been trying to articulate for a while.

> Regularly drinking within the recommended guideline amount can still have a negative effect on one's mental health. Sometimes people are very busy and drink in order to relax or in order to temporarily brighten up their mood, but essentially they're replacing an uncomfortable emotional state with a more pleasant one. The problem here is that people then subconsciously start learning to fear their own emotions, which only makes their inner tension stronger. This of course promotes more avoidance strategies and therefore creates a negative cycle that can be very hard to get out of.

Peter's quote touches on one of the most fundamental things I have learned since being sober, which is that good mental health comes from facing and getting through testing times without a drink to 'take the edge off'. Good mental health comes from the real confidence you build every time you make it through an uncomfortable situation without the aid of booze, so that the next time something equally daunting comes along, you know that you can conquer it because you've done so before. The pressure of edges and feelings of discomfort are what cause us to transform and adapt. Edges are a good thing, and the most rewarding experiences always lie just beyond our comfort zone.

So, while units are there to curb the physical dangers of our drinking, are they really taking into account the effect a few glasses of wine every time we're remotely stressed could be having on our mental health?

Short Term vs. Long Term

Sitting with your feelings sounds all well and good, but it does take a lot of work, and unfortunately we're suckers for quick fixes. We are, after all, a culture of instant gratification. We're all guilty of it. We vow to invest in local businesses and shop small, but before we know it we're ordering from Amazon Prime because we need it and we need it *now*. While there's a time and a place for this, it's a sign of us opting for the easy solution, the quick fix, and not necessarily the thing that will do us (or others) good in the long run. In the case of alcohol, this means alleviating stress with a bottle of pinot rather than working through any kind of slightly uncomfortable emotion.

Here are a few science-backed tools that are proven to crush cravings for booze as well as promote good mental health. None of them are quick fixes, but some are definitely speedier than others.

Exercise

A study published in the January 2015 issue of the *American Journal of Drug and Alcohol Abuse* found that regular aerobic exercise does curb alcohol dependence and cravings among those who are in the early stages of recovery.[3] Founder of London exercise studio Barreworks, Vicki Anstey, says that 'cardio can lead to increased anxiety with increased heart rate, so opt for resistance or strength training.'

Mindfulness

A University College London study published in the *International Journal of Neuropsychopharmacology* showed that just eleven minutes of mindfulness training helps drinkers cut back. After an eleven-minute training session and encouragement to continue practising mindfulness (which involves focusing on what's happening in the present moment), heavy drinkers drank less over the subsequent week than people who were taught relaxation techniques.[4]

CBT

Not to be confused with CBD, CBT (cognitive behavioural therapy) is one of the most popular and successful treatments for alcohol-use disorder. It focuses on challenging and changing unhelpful behaviour and developing personal coping strategies. It's definitely more work than exercise and mindfulness, but from a personal perspective it changed my life.

If you're still a quick-fix fan or need something more immediate, then herbal teas, essential oils, guided meditations and yes, bubble baths are all helpful for relaxing and promoting sleep and therefore positive mental wellbeing, which, in turn, can foster a stronger resolve for turning down the drink. They're also cheaper than wine!

Anti-depressants

If you're already taking anti-depressants, it's worth doing some extra research around this subject and speaking to your doctor, but the NHS guidance is that it's generally not advised to drink alcohol while taking this kind of medication. Why? Well, alcohol is a depressant and decreases the serotonin levels in our brain while anti-depressants are designed to increase them. What this means is that by drinking alcohol, you're decreasing the effectiveness of your medication to the point where you may experience extreme lows.

Drinking alcohol with anti-depressants can even create a whole load of unpleasant side effects, some of which – such as fatigue – actually mimic symptoms of depression, so you may start to feel like they're not working and you don't feel better at all. There is some speculation that mixing anti-depressants with alcohol could even increase your chances of blackouts.

If all you've taken from this is that you need to stop taking your meds so that you can go on a bender, please don't. The NHS is very clear that you should never stop taking anti-depressant medication just so you can drink alcohol, as this can cause withdrawal effects such as flu-like symptoms, sensations in the body that feel like electric shocks, and fits.

Other Conditions

It's still unclear with a lot of mental health disorders what is cause and what is effect when it comes to alcohol consumption. For conditions such as bipolar and obsessive compulsive disorder, alcohol is thought to worsen symptoms, but for a lot of people it might offer an initial numbing relief, and so cycles can form that are harder to untangle. If you do have mental health issues, self-medicating with alcohol is not the answer and it's important to seek advice from a medical professional.

Sober Girl Spotlight

'Sobriety makes managing my mental health easier.'

Self-love blogger and YouTuber Olivia Callaghan (@selfloveliv) gave up drinking in 2019 after she noticed that alcohol was exacerbating her bipolar disorder, which she was diagnosed with in 2011. Liv started having panic attacks on nights out and began to use alcohol as a crutch.

Alcohol was definitely affecting my mental health. I'd normally feel fine during the actual drinking, so it felt like it was helping, but as soon as I woke up in the morning I'd feel depressed, and often suicidal. Unbeknown to me at the time, I was making everything worse.

Now, with a clear head and more regulated emotions, Liv says that she is much better equipped at managing her mental health, something she does with medication, therapy and being open with her friends and family.

Sobriety is scary at first, especially when you've relied on alcohol for so long, but your health matters, and that includes your mental health. Put yourself first, don't feel pressured to drink if you choose not to, and remember, you got this, boo!

Self-harm

A 2015 study concluded that alcohol use and misuse in self-harm patients appears to have increased in recent years, particularly in women, and that the association of alcohol with greater risk of self-harm repetition and mortality highlights the need for clinicians to investigate alcohol use in self-harm patients.[5] The link between the two, however, seems to be unclear. Perhaps it's because alcohol makes us more impulsive, or perhaps it's because it gives us the courage to do things we can't do sober. Either way, the link is there.

Suicide

A 2010 paper entitled 'Suicidal Behaviour and Alcohol Abuse' reached the following conclusion:[6]

> Suicide is the result of complex interactions between biological, psychological, social and environmental factors, and all of these conditions impact on one another. Environmental stressors act on a genetically determined and environmentally modulated physical structure that in turn impacts psychological wellbeing and may cause a psychiatric illness that affects the person's inner world and paves the way for suicide. Alcohol abuse is a means of easing one's psychological stress but, at the same time, impacts on all other factors, rendering suicide more likely.

The paper stated that programmes for suicide prevention must take into account drinking habits and should reinforce healthy behavioural patterns.

In the space of three years, two contestants on the ITV2 show *Love Island* died by suicide. In the cases of Mike Thalassitis and Sophie Gradon, their toxicology reports showed that they both had taken mixtures of alcohol and cocaine before their deaths.

At Sophie's hearing, the coroner ruled that US evidence has shown that the combination of alcohol and cocaine can make you sixteen times more likely to take your own life. He went on to say that the former Miss Great Britain would not have acted as she did if she had not taken that combination of drugs, which made her behave irrationally:

The combination I am given to understand is used by those who believe it brings on a so-called high much quicker. What they may not appreciate is it is also now thought to give rise to violent thoughts, and those thoughts can be against the self. If Sophie's death is to serve any purpose at all, that message should go out far and wide.

I don't believe it's my place to comment on whether these deaths could have been prevented, but I feel like it would be irresponsible of me to have this platform and not follow the coroner's advice to pass on this information.

Pink Clouds

There's a phenomenon discussed in sobriety circles known as 'pink cloud', which is said to be the temporary stage of elation and excitement when you first quit drinking. The theory is that the 'fog' has lifted and everything feels fluffy and lovely, but there is a warning when it comes to pink clouds: they will usually, at some point, disperse. My pink-cloud phase lasted four months.

In June 2018, I came back from a trip to Canada and began to feel very weird. I could tell something wasn't right. It all started with feeling like I wasn't really in the room when people were talking to me, and then it moved on to me not feeling like I had control of my own body. Everything felt either supersonic or as if I was under water. On some days, I felt devoid of emotion to the point where someone could have told me that I really did have cancer and it wouldn't have fazed me at all. On other days I couldn't stop sobbing uncontrollably and was having panic attacks every other hour.

I remember someone giving me a plant pot to hold one day. I held out my arms to take it but I couldn't make my hands grip it. I just remember watching it fall in slow motion and smash on the floor. I barely reacted other than to mumble an offer to clear it up. When things like this happened, I convinced myself that something was wrong with me physically, that perhaps I had a brain tumour or my body was slowly shutting down. I took myself to the doctor, who told me I didn't have a brain tumour and that I was probably just anxious – a diagnosis that, at the time, made me furious.

Sometimes I'd be in a room and it would spin to the point where I felt physically sick. Other times I wondered if I was seeing life as a ghost, and on my darkest day I wished I could actually die. This strange series of events continued for two months until one day I cried in the middle of my office because I felt overwhelmed by how loud everyone's typing was, including my own. I told my boss that I just didn't feel right and she told me to take some time off. Lara, if you read this – that was the kindest reaction and I will never forget it.

Throughout it all, I had a very weird feeling that I needed to stay sober, and looking back, I still think it's nothing short of a miracle that I succeeded. Though in some ways, drinking was the last thing on my mind while I was feeling like that. After being sent home from work, my mum found me the number of a local therapist and I started going twice a week.

My therapist lived two roads along from me and I remember walking there for my first session and wondering what I would say other than 'my brain is broken'. I was still half convinced I was suffering from a very serious disease.

Therapy is expensive and I get that not everyone is in a position to pay for professional help. If you're struggling financially there are free and low-cost options available, which I've included in the support and resources section at the back of this book (see page 288). I also want to point out that therapy is not supposed to be Instagrammable. I went to someone local, who worked from her spare room rather than from a big fancy office, because I couldn't afford the rates being charged in central London and my mum had to help me out with the fees. Therapy doesn't need to involve you lying on a chaise longue surrounded by oak bookshelves to be effective.

I went for twice-weekly sessions for three months, but even after two sessions of CBT I started to understand what was going on in my brain. Essentially, what I believe happened was this. For eight years, I had numbed every single negative emotion with booze – from stress and heartbreak to anger and insecurity. As a newly sober human, there I was dealing with it all at once. For the first time in my life, I was learning how to process emotion and it seems like my body was so overwhelmed by the whole idea that it would selectively check out at points.

My friends and family deserve a mention here for being truly amazing during that time. A shout-out to Shauna, who took me for both reiki and a colonic irrigation on the same day in an attempt to help me. The mark of a true friend is someone who will sit with you in a room while you get seven-year-old poo suctioned from your bowels.

I don't talk about my breakdown a lot. Sometimes I worry it might scare people off sobriety because they believe it might unleash decades of suppressed feelings, but my 'blip' is, without a doubt, the most drastic positive turning point in my life – probably even above choosing to embrace sobriety.

It's when I learned how to deal with my feelings and emotions. It's when I learned that good mental health is not about being happy 24/7, but about how you process your emotions. So, just a word of warning – make sure you have some tools in place for when or if (some people stay fluffy) your pink cloud disperses, especially if you think a lot might come up for you when you decide to bin the booze.

Sobriety Is Not a Magic Mental Health Wand

I've heard a few people liken sobriety to having an Instagram filter because everything suddenly looks so sparkly and wonderful. In my opinion, it's the complete opposite. Everything is always very real in sobriety. There are no blurred lines, nothing is softened, and nothing is edited, tweaked or made more appealing to the eye. The edge is never taken off. Everything is raw and, most importantly, authentic. It's a photo that doesn't necessarily look good, but is 100 per cent true to life.

These days when I cry, it's a real sob that I feel deeply, not shallow tears about a drunken argument. That's not to say I don't blub like a baby at trivial things such as dog movies. In fact, I cry more now because I'm so in tune with my emotions. I cry more and yet I'm the happiest I've ever been. When I connect with someone, it's a physical energy that I can actually feel – the conversations are honest and free from the bravado of booze. I get a genuine thrill when someone opens my mind to a new way of thinking. I divulge my darkest secrets to make genuine connections and share my experience rather than because I'm intoxicated and sharing out of guilt or shame.

Sobriety is not going to solve all your problems, especially when it comes to mental health, and for a while things might feel really shitty. Ultimately, sobriety is now a tool that I use to make everything (including my emotions) more manageable. Lots of things feel harder when they're real, but they're also more rewarding. Meeting people for the first time is more nerve-racking but more exciting; first kisses are more awkward but more meaningful; hard days are more challenging but more beneficial for emotional growth. For me, all of this – the messiness, the vulnerability and the imperfection – is the real sparkle. I really want you to know that sobriety isn't going to make everything perfect but the best things never are.

Sober Girl Gains

☐ No more hangover anxiety

☐ Say goodbye to shame

☐ A good gut that's got your back

☐ Retirement from the Blackout Investigation Bureau

☐ Healthier coping mechanisms for dealing with the shittier times

5

Get Well Soon

Alcohol and the eight pillars of wellness

While wellness is certainly not a one-size-fits-all kind of deal, there are a few models around that try to best explain how each and every one of us can lead both healthier and all-round happier lives. In 2016, the US-based Substance Abuse and Mental Health Services Administration (SAMHSA) rolled out an initiative that identified eight dimensions of wellness which, if focused on, are thought to optimize your overall wellbeing. They are:

- ♥ Physical wellness

- ♥ Emotional wellness

- ♥ Spiritual wellness

- ♥ Financial wellness

- ♥ Social wellness

♥ Environmental wellness

♥ Intellectual wellness

♥ Occupational wellness

Looking at wellbeing from such a holistic perspective completely resonates with me, because I honestly don't believe that doing a one-time thing will suddenly cure all your problems and put you in high spirits. I do believe, however, that optimum wellbeing comes from improving all aspects of our lives – a kind of 360-approach, if you will. The good news is that while sobriety might seem like an isolated decision (a passing phase such as a juice cleanse or a yoni egg), simply removing alcohol from your life can cause a domino effect of positive repercussions.

An all-encompassing approach to wellness is not meant to sound overwhelming. I am by no means suggesting that to be deemed 'well' you need to run a triathlon, adopt a vegan lifestyle and go to inspirational talks three times a month, but it is about making small changes in different areas of your life that can make a bigger impact overall.

Much like therapy, this approach to wellness does not need to look good for the 'Gram (that's Instagram to you, Mum). It is inclusive, not exclusive. To be well you do not need to eat over-priced quinoa, wear designer yoga leggings or attend classes at a fancy spin studio. Eating odd-sized veg from Lidl, wearing your pjs until they're baggy, or taking some quiet time at the end of the day will tick all the same boxes.

Something key to keep in mind when it comes to how sobriety links to wellness, especially in this model, is that the whole thing works as a two-way street. Removing alcohol will almost instantly have an impact on every single one of these eight pillars of well-being in a positive way, but similarly, by improving these dimensions independently you will begin to create an existence that is conducive to making sobriety work too.

You will probably find that you start to create a life you love so much that you won't want to numb or quieten it. Quite the opposite will happen. You will want to fully embrace it and be present for it every single day.

If you are here because you are sober curious and the thought of eliminating or drastically reducing alcohol from your existence feels overwhelming and too much like an immediate all-or-nothing move, then my advice is to perhaps improve your wellbeing in these areas first in order to reach a point where your life feels abundant enough without it. Then (and you'll probably find it happens naturally) you can slowly start to take drinking out of the equation because it no longer fits in with everything else.

Looking at most alcohol-based research papers, the focus tends to be on the physiological and psychological harms of alcohol, which suggests these are the areas of our wellbeing where science believes drinking has the most detrimental effect. It's also why you've just read two chapters dedicated to your mental and physical health. It therefore makes sense to start improving these areas first, by putting in place some of the more obvious tools – such as exercise and nutritional eating – and the other healthier coping mechanisms we discussed in Chapter Four. This will provide good foundations for improving your wellbeing in other areas.

Here is where I am going to dive into the rest of the pillars and show you why binning the booze can impact all areas of your life, from sustainability to your savings, and how you can use everything from crystals to cleaning to keep you on track.

Spiritual Wellness

This dimension isn't all reiki and moon cycles (though both will be mentioned), it's more about your values, beliefs and finding your purpose in the world. If this sounds like a lot of pious soul-searching, don't worry – a few things happen straight away when you stop drinking that don't involve having to download your birth chart to figure out your rising sign.

For me, being sober means that I am more aligned with my own morals, and I hold up my end of the bargain with both others and myself. Drunk me cared very little for my moral compass. In fact, anything I believed to be the 'right thing' went completely out the window after two proseccos and a tequila when drunk Millie took hold.

Drunk Millie was arrogant, selfish, spiteful and hedonistic. She flirted with people she shouldn't have, did things she shouldn't have, and said things she shouldn't have. Whenever I woke up the morning after a big night out, I always felt so ashamed of her behaviour and the trail of mass destruction she left wherever she went. Sometimes I even felt as if I had an evil twin trapped inside me, and blacking out meant that I rarely remembered what drunk Millie had done. I always felt like I was clearing up some-one else's mess.

For a long time, I didn't own my mistakes because I was too ashamed of them, and more importantly they didn't feel like mine because I couldn't believe I was capable of such things. Instead, I just blamed it on my evil twin. Drunk Millie, the Mr Hyde to my Dr Jekyll. I think this caused me to experience a lot of disconnect because I felt like I was trying to shun a large part of myself – a self-loathing monster that lived inside of me and came out after three drinks. I constantly struggled with an inner moralistic battle in which I wondered whether I was truly a good person or not. How could I be a decent human when I did such outrageous things?

Enhancing your connection to yourself is a key part of the spiritual dimension, and thanks to sobriety I am finally able to accept and connect with every part of myself. I have even come to accept the bits that I don't like, because at least I know they are me and not orchestrated by a rampaging, tequila-fuelled demon who seemed rather hell-bent on ruining my life.

Essentially, what I now know is that alcohol interferes with the part of your brain that helps you make decisions and under- stand the difference between right and wrong. We'll discuss this in a little more detail in Chapter Seven, in the context of cheating. Without this part of the brain functioning fully, you tend to turn a little primal. You want to shag, fight and eat more with very little care in the world for the consequences. Drunk me wasn't a monster, she was a cavewoman who hadn't evolved.

Still, even if she wasn't the devil in disguise, I still prefer that my actions now align with the things I believe in. This doesn't mean I don't make mistakes, but I know that everything I do comes from a good place with similarly good intentions: never to hurt the people I care about, never to hurt strangers, and never to hurt myself.

One thing I find when I talk to SGS girls is that shame is quite a common theme in our discussions. Forgiving yourself for the things that you did when you were drinking is a massive part of the healing process in sobriety. After all, getting into a sort of shame-cycle – feeling ashamed about things you did when you were drunk and so drinking to stop feeling that way – is a big reason why a lot of us continue to drink.

When it comes to self-forgiveness, it's worth reading around the subject (Maya Angelou penned some of my favourite words of wisdom in this area) but most of the advice goes along the lines of realizing you are human and therefore going to make mistakes, and seeing these occasions as opportunities to learn and make amends.

I genuinely believe that sobriety has made me an all-round nicer person and a better human. I am always ready to show up, absorb and act. I have more time to educate myself on important issues and understand what's going on in the world. It's impossible to go on some kind of spiritual journey without first unpacking and understanding concepts such as intersectionality and issues such as systems of oppression.

Every day I am trying to be a better person, and for me, sobriety (or more the absence of drinking and hangovers) accelerates that growth. There's nothing like constantly having a clear head for self-reflection and contemplating the universe without the option to selectively check out.

One thing I've noticed is that my tendency to gossip toxically happens far less frequently now that I never feel uninhibited after a few glasses of wine. Again, this book is not about pretending that I'm a virtuous angel, but these days I'm far more likely to check myself if I find I'm caught up in conversations about other people which are, in fact, none of my business.

As well as enhancing your connection to yourself, another part of the spiritual dimension is enhancing your connection to nature. Using my hangover-free time to get outside more and delight in the sun on my face feels more important to me than it ever did before. I've definitely found a strange new appreciation of natural beauty in the world. I like it when it rains, I love watching sunsets, and even sitting on grass fills me with a sense of calm and oneness with the world.

When it comes to the more New Age (though really, they're old age) side of things, I've realized that removing alcohol from my life has definitely made me more open to being a little more spiritual. Some people believe that alcohol can lower your vibration, create holes in your aura and numb your psychic senses – so the theory goes that, without it, you're more attuned to the energy of the world.

If you need a little outside help to strengthen your sobriety journey and you're feeling open-minded, there are a few tools that you can use.

Crystals

Not only do they look pretty, but crystals also have powerful healing properties. If you're rolling your eyes right now, bear with me, because there is some science behind it. Natural crystals vibrate with energy, and that's why we use them in everything from medical lasers to very expensive watches.

Traditionally, amethyst is thought to be the sober stone – its name comes from the Greek word *amethystos*, meaning 'not drunken' – but there are a host of other stones that could help you too: rutilated quartz is said to help you make important life changes; mookaite is associated with cosmic rebirth, allowing you to release the weight of your past; and malachite promotes assertiveness, strength and owning your individualism. For more reading on crystals, check out my recommendations in the support and resources section (see page 281).

The Moon

As we all know, the moon is responsible for the tides – which means it somehow manages to move entire oceans! As human beings, we are made of up to 60 per cent water, so is it silly to ignore the effect the moon could be having on us? After all, the word 'lunatic' comes from the Latin word *lunaticus*, meaning 'moonstruck', which refers to madness caused by the moon. The moral is, check in with the lunar cycles, especially when it comes to a full moon, which is thought to affect sleep patterns. You'll know to be a little kinder to yourself during these times.

Yoga

Yes, it's wonderful for our physical wellness to have a good old stretch, but yoga has very spiritual origins and the practice itself is thought to cultivate awareness and self-regulation. Yoga is not something you need to be perfect at, it's about finding inner calm and alignment. Sober yoga teacher Mel Hamilton (@rebelsobriety on Instagram) has some great yoga videos to get you started, and she also does alcohol-free beer reviews too!

Other things worth looking into are reiki, acupuncture, astrology and, of course, the big one, faith. Reiki works to heal and release trauma from the body via energy, acupuncture can help relieve cravings, and astrology (I appreciate this one might feel far-fetched) can help you to understand your own cosmic blueprint. Lots of people connect (or reconnect) with faith in sobriety and, as we now know, those working the AA steps often find connection with a higher power that doesn't need to be religious at all.

Financial Wellness

The morning after a night of drinking, I would actively avoid checking my bank account. I never knew how much I'd spent, because I genuinely couldn't remember, but I always knew it would be somewhere between shocking and horrifying. Of course, I would then do the super-sensible thing and splash more cash by ordering a KFC or making frivolous ASOS purchases in an effort to lift my spirits. Needless to say, alcohol made me financially very 'unwell', and that is why I am a 29-year-old woman writing this book from her parents' house.

Luckily, sobriety has finally allowed me to get on top of my finances, and I hope that at some point soon I'll be the proud owner of my own flat, something that four years ago, while eating bacon from a pan and pulling out a reel of Jägerbomb receipts from my purse, would have seemed quite laughable.

A survey by Macmillan Cancer Support showed that the average Brit spends around £787 a year on alcohol (with Londoners spending slightly more).[1] Honestly, to me that sounds a little modest. Still, if we go by this estimation, then Macmillan warned it means that over the course of their lifetime, the average Briton spends about £50,000 on alcohol.

When we talk about these numbers, I think it's interesting to discuss the fact that what we're really referring to is the direct cost of the alcohol itself, but what about all the indirect costs? I know from experience that I've saved a fortune now that I no longer need taxis home after missing my last train or replacement phones for the ones I lost. I asked my followers what they had saved money on, and here are just some of the answers:

'Uber cleaning fees because I no longer vomit.'

'Hangover food.'

'Replacement phones.'

'Having to take "sick" days which I'm not paid for.'

'Cigarettes.'

'Replacing ripped and stained clothes.'

'Buying apology presents for people after I was a dick to them.'

'Bank overdraft fees.'

'Ibuprofen.'

'Taxis to see horrible men on the other side of London.' (Been there.)

'Random things that I would order online drunk.'

'Rides to work because I was too hungover for public transport.'

'Replacing my ID/passport.'

'Impulse events like deciding to go on holiday with people from the pub.'

'Food bought during a night out.'

'Replacement make-up.'

'Locksmiths after losing my keys.'

I'll be honest and admit that in my first six months of sobriety I barely saved a penny. Not only was I paying off my hefty overdraft, but I was also so shocked to have money left over at the end of the month that I spent it on extravagant solo holidays, books and replacing all the fag-burned dresses in my wardrobe with brand-new, shiny garments (you can generally wear more white once you're sober, FYI).

I have absolutely no regrets about those purchases and neither should you. Having something to show for my sobriety rather than savings felt really important to me at the time, and I know that those books and holidays did more for my sobriety than money in the bank ever could. After those initial splurges I managed to rein in my spending – though I still find myself excusing the odd purchase as a reward for being alcohol-free.

Slowly but surely my finances are recovering from the dent made in them by years of quite literally pissing my money up the wall. While I don't think I'll be giving Jeff Bezos a run for his money any time soon, I'm happy to report that I no longer live pay day to pay day, and this is enough for me to consider myself financially 'well'. Sobriety has allowed me to develop better financial habits and plan for the future.

Sober Girl Spotlight
'Sobriety has made me more money confident!'

Mindset coach and TV producer Ella St John McGrand (@ellastjohnmcgrand) gave up drinking in 2019 and saved

£2,500 in her first year of sobriety: 'Stopping drinking has made me more mindful of how I spend money, and has given me more confidence to ask for higher rates when working in TV.'

Ella gave up drinking while training to be a coach as she realized that it was making her miserable. After years of binge-drinking and a sobriety stint of six months, what made sobriety stick for good was Ella's ability to address the deeper issue of why she was drinking: 'I was at a friend's hen do when the penny finally dropped – alcohol was never going to make me feel good. I had told myself for years that I wasn't good enough. At that moment I knew that belief had to change.'

Within her first year of sobriety, Ella went on to work on high-profile history documentaries and also set up her own coaching business on the side. She says sobriety gave her the self-awareness to spot when she's likely to overspend on clothes, and she's now supporting women to manage their money in her coaching programmes. 'Talk about an ROI, sobriety is the best investment you will make for your money!'

Social Wellness

Don't panic, this one isn't about being the biggest social butterfly – though if you're up for spreading your sober wings, then fly, my pretties. Social wellness is about finding a sense of connection and belonging with others, as well as developing a good support system for the trickier times in life when you might feel yourself slip/question your decision.

Luckily, I have a whole chapter on friendship for you coming up, including why sobriety has made me a better friend, and how you can make new mates in your area too. In terms of this one being a two-way street, I am absolutely a better friend now that I'm sober, and in return my friendships are more supportive, which has helped to strengthen my sobriety. I've also found a sense of belonging in the SGS community, which has been instrumental for flourishing in my alcohol-free life.

Some initial things to consider when it comes to social wellness are trying to make at least one social connection daily (I highly recommend a phone call at the very least) and reflecting on what your social needs really are – how can you meet them? What do you need to gain from interactions? It's also important to work out what socializing looks like for you now that you're sober, to ensure that you don't self-isolate and cut yourself off completely.

Social wellness also means not hesitating to seek help from others, so working to break down some of those vulnerability barriers is key. Don't be afraid to lean on others when you need support – there's no shame in admitting that you cannot handle things on your own.

Environmental Wellness

This dimension is all about curating an environment that supports your wellbeing, and can include everything from your immediate surroundings to the wider world. Sobriety has definitely allowed me to deal with what's in front of me, even if that means just taking time to clean, tidy or declutter Marie Kondo-style to provide a more calming environment. It's also helped me to be a little more conscious of the wider world.

While I certainly didn't care about reusable cups when I was hungover and desperate for caffeine, I am far more conscientious about making more sustainable choices now. Again, I am by no means perfect, but as chef Anne-Marie Bonneau puts it, 'We don't need a handful of people doing zero waste perfectly. We need millions of people doing it imperfectly.'

Environmental wellness is about feeling safe in your environment and establishing surroundings which encourage good physical and mental health, and in this case are conducive to you being alcohol-free. This might include setting boundaries, which we'll discuss in later chapters, but if those prove ineffective then you might have to remove yourself from a living situation or job altogether, providing that it is an option available to you.

Intellectual Wellness

This dimension of wellness is all about expanding your knowledge; becoming a lifelong learner; finding things and creative outlets that stimulate you; and being open to new ideas and wisdom.

We have a long-running joke at SGS that you take up so many random hobbies in early sobriety that you come out of it as a salsa-dancing botanist who can crochet and read tarot cards – it really is quite true! Sobriety gives you the time and energy to take up new interests and learn new skills. In turn, those things can offer fulfilment and help you to stay sober.

As well as taking up a whole load of new hobbies, I've found that sobriety has led me to reconnect with old ones – things that I enjoyed before drinking became my default activity when it came to having a good time.

As I mentioned, up until the age of eighteen competitive dancing was pretty much my life, but when I went to university my passion for dancing was swiftly replaced with my passion for drinking, so I stopped taking it seriously. I rarely came home for practice, and even turned up to one competition so hungover that I didn't notice when my top snapped and I basically danced around with my boobs out. Eventually I stopped dancing altogether.

When I stopped drinking, one of the first things I did was go back to dance classes. Despite not being as good as I used to be, I remembered immediately how happy something as simple as moving my limbs made me feel. It was the kind of happy that has no rhyme or reason to it, but you just feel it and it just is.

Dancing isn't the only thing I've reconnected with. Since becoming sober I've embraced my inner child by jumping on more trampolines, playing in arcades, and for my last birthday I made everyone go to our local theme park. With my hand on my heart I can say that the last three, alcohol-free years of my life have been the happiest.

Whatever you reconnect with doesn't have to be fancy, and it doesn't have to be a big passion, you can just seek out the little things that you used to love doing. Simple joys, such as moving your body or throwing a bowling ball, can contribute to a much bigger sense of pleasure – one that you probably used to have before you ever even picked up a drink.

One thing I am absolutely passionate about – and one of the easiest ways to boost brain power – is reading, and fortunately there's a whole host of books that can challenge your thinking about drinking and beyond. I've listed my favourite titles in the support and resources section (see pages 279–289), including the best 'quit lit' memoirs and some books that have nothing to do with booze but are ones I think can indirectly strengthen your sobriety and help you handle the other stuff that might be leading you to seek comfort in alcohol. For anyone with a preference for audio, I've also included the best sobriety-themed podcasts for your listening pleasure.

Occupational Wellness

This dimension is a little trickier because it involves a lot of musings around job satisfaction, and a lot of people don't exactly thrive on what they're doing for employment. What I will say is that more often than not sobriety makes you a better employee (not turning up late, always being relatively alert, and so on) and sometimes being a good employee will come with some nice little perks, such as pay rises and promotions. Not embarrassing yourself at work parties is also hugely valuable and I'll let you know how to survive one sober later!

Occupational wellness also looks to help you invest in the things that you're passionate about, even if that doesn't include your day job, and this is where sobriety has come in handy for me.

Before sobriety I really liked my job, but I wouldn't say it fulfilled me. Working for a magazine and writing about the best budget clothes is super fun, but after a while it stopped lighting my soul on fire. Getting sober allowed me the time and freedom to start the Sober Girl Society, and having a passion project really gave me a new sense of purpose and something to do other than drinking. Granted, it's all about sobriety, but yours doesn't have to be, and I know plenty of other women who have gone back into education, trained for a new job or started a side hustle because of the focus they gained when they ditched alcohol.

Considering volunteer work or getting involved with a charity is another great way to boost your wellness in this area. If you have a cause you are passionate about, or something you want to change, now is a great time to work on it, and social media is such an accessible platform for getting started. It doesn't have to be something massive either; while I'm sure many of us have dreams of changing the world on a global scale, there's plenty to be done in your local community. If sobriety is your passion, then we'll have plenty of tips later on how you can help be a part of the alcohol-free movement and campaign for sober inclusivity.

With all that said, please do not feel the pressure to become the most productive person alive just because you're sober. Learning how to navigate a life without alcohol is a mammoth task in itself, so if you want to sit in your pyjamas and watch television all day, I fully support your decision.

Well, Well, Well . . .

Ultimately, it all comes down to this: sobriety (or at the very least sober curiosity) gives you a better chance of increasing your optimum wellbeing, and that gives you a better chance of sticking with it in the long term. Taking alcohol off the table has allowed me to put more time and energy towards improving my own eight pillars of wellness, which has helped me create a full and happy life in which I now feel that drinking would only be to its detriment.

Sober Girl Gains

☐ Money in the bank

☐ A host of new hobbies

☐ An extensive library

☐ A hole-free aura

☐ An increased sense of overall wellness

PART THREE

Navigating the New Normal

6

On Wednesdays We Don't Drink

Friendship, nights out and bottomless brunches

I am your typical girl's girl. I am in no way ashamed to admit that I am a basic brunch bitch and a proud feminist. I have been to more hen parties and baby showers than I can count, and I am constantly in awe of the amazing and incredible women I meet on a daily basis, sober or otherwise.

I want to point this out because for a long time I loved the idea of being different to other women. Obsessed by seeking validation from men, and in the hope that they would see me as 'the cool girl', I'd often make wild declarations about how much I loved football, when the reality is that I couldn't give an actual feck about it. I'd scoff about girls who were obsessed with their hair and make-up while failing to acknowledge the fact that I owned at least seven shades of nude lipsticks and three different heated hair tools.

Unfortunately, I don't think I'm alone in this. When pop royalty Hailee Steinfeld released her single 'Most Girls' in 2017, she did an interview with the *Guardian* in which she talked about this bizarre, unspoken rule we seem to have, where to be special you have to be different to other women,* which is why her catchy song is aimed at counteracting this culture of treating one another as competition, and encourages us to collectively empower each other as women instead.

You might notice men say things in films like, 'You're not like other girls.' I used to take it as a compliment, but it's now something I take offence at. Let me tell you now: to be special, you do not need to be better than other women. I am special because all women are. I am probably a bit like you, and you are more than likely a bit like me, and there is nothing wrong with being like other girls – because we're simply the best.

I truly believe that friendships are as – if not more – important than romantic relationships, and I also believe that I wouldn't have made it through some of the harder moments in my life without the help of the superwomen I am absolutely blessed to call my friends.

You might be wondering why I'm divulging the fact that I love girl power more than the Spice Girls, so I'll tell you what I want (what I really, really want) and that is for you to believe me when I say that worrying about how my friendships would change if I gave up drinking was my absolute main fear. If it's yours too, I hope this chapter will show you why being the sober pal is *not* amazingly shit and that friendship never ends . . . even when you're sober!

---

* Google 'internalized misogyny'.

BFF (Boozy Friends for Ever)

It's been said that 'fear' is an acronym for 'false evidence appearing real', so here's the thing when it comes to alcohol and friendship – the false evidence is everywhere. Just a quick Google search of friendship quotes will fill your screen with boozy BFF mantras that include but are definitely not limited to:

> *'A true friend reaches for your hand and puts a wine glass in it.'*
>
> *'Friends for ever through thick and gin.'*
>
> *'Friends are therapists you can drink with.'*

And my personal favourite . . .

> *'If you don't drink, how will your friends know that you love them at 2 a.m.?'*

Despite the fact that I used to share these as memes (and I'm pretty sure I had one emblazoned on a birthday card), I have some small but very important spoiler alerts for you:

♥ It is enough for a true friend to *just* reach for your hand and not put anything in it.

♥ You can be friends through thick and *thin*.

♥ Friends are positively biased towards you, and therefore make truly horrible therapists.

♥ Finally, if you really want your friends to know that you love them, then you can just tell them at 2 p.m. instead.

But it's not just these cutesy mottos that are pushing booze as a bonder, because the idea that alcohol is at the centre of all good friendships is everywhere. It's plastered over social media with boomerangs of clinking glasses; it's in magazines with cocktail recipes for a girls' night in; it's essentially the whole narrative of Netflix's gal-pal film *Wine Country*; it's pretty much the core premise of *Sex and the City*; and it's even in song lyrics.

Little Mix have a single based on the strength of female support that offers up wine and make-up wipes to their heartbroken friend; and although Jermaine Stewart is adamant that we don't have to take our clothes off to have a good time, he does insist that we must all drink cherry wine.

When I hear these songs, it really affirms just how much this idea about alcohol has seeped into our contemporary culture; that most people believe that fun and supportive friendships are based upon flavoured booze, drunk dancing and face wipes. Believe me when I say there is no judgement here, because this is the narrative that I believed for *so* long too.

Apart from a few faithful school pals and the friends I met through dancing, my main circle of besties consists of the ones that I made later in life, at university. This means that not only was alcohol a shared interest, but it was also the thing that brought us together and solidified our place in each other's lives in the first place. A boozy Freshers' Week pub crawl around Brighton town and a game where we all had to state our favourite sex positions was all it took for us to know that we'd be in each other's lives for a very long time. I remember distinctly having extra respect for my friend Emma when she told me that just three weeks before starting uni, she was carried out of Pacha nightclub in London by paramedics for being too drunk.

For the eleven years that we've been mates, I was drinking for eight of those, and even after we left university every celebration was a bottomless brunch, a night out dedicated to our shared interest of getting hammered, or a day spent drinking in my garden for the annual festival I aptly named Goochella – BYOB.

This meant that when I initially thought about ditching the drink for good, I had two major concerns about how it would affect the friendships in my life. The first was that I assumed this would be the end of life with my existing pals as I knew it. No more Goochella, no more brunch and no more laughter. The second was that without a shared interest of alcohol to unite us, I'd never bond or make friends with another human being again.

It turns out I was half right about the first one. It was the end of life as I knew it with my friends, but my friendships have evolved beyond recognition in only positive ways. They're more beautiful, complex and colourful than I ever imagined they would be. Goochella still takes place each year, I'm still as brunched up as ever, and if anything I laugh more than I did before. I've learned that despite what songwriters and the inspirational quotes on the internet might tell you, a bottle of pinot grigio isn't the only way to support a friend in crisis. In fact, a much better way to be there for someone is to show up, and I don't just mean turn up – I mean really show up. Physically, mentally and emotionally. To listen deeply and to understand.

Sobriety has allowed me to do that: to be the best friend I can possibly be, supporting my friends through their heartbreak, job losses, grief, and even just the weeks when they're extra hormonal and need someone to listen. I've learned that you can turn up at their house without a bottle of the supermarket's finest plonk and just giving them a comforting embrace is enough. Lest we forget that wine – or any alcohol, for that matter – is a depressant in a bottle, it seems bizarre that the way we choose to help our vulnerable friends through tough times is to bring them something that will potentially just make them sadder.

Sobriety also means I no longer cancel plans. I'm not labelled as the flaky friend any more, or the one who's a 'little bit of a liability'. I can't even begin to count the number of times when drinking or subsequent hangovers resulted in me bailing on things at the eleventh hour or, against all odds, managing to turn up, but still being too hungover to actually function as a good friend or an effective human.

I always remember the Easter when my friend Gabbi organized a gathering at her house. I knew it was important, so despite being on the brink of vomiting after I'd been out until 6 a.m., I dragged myself over to hers. When I eventually got there, after a rather distressing tube journey, I could barely speak. My friends all sat around the table while I curled up on the sofa, disintegrating slowly. I didn't eat anything, I didn't contribute anything. I might as well not have been there. I was in charge of organizing the Easter egg hunt and I'd pathetically organized . . . fuck all. I still feel bad about all the effort that went into that day and the complete lack of reciprocation from me.

When I turn up to events now, I'm caring and attentive. Instead of heading straight to the bar at a birthday party or asking the host of the baby shower if there's any prosecco, I offer to help. I ask if I can lend a hand with the food or the washing up, or I'll offer to drive someone's nan home. When I cry at my friends' engagement parties it's out of happiness and not because I've necked three tequilas and I'm feeling sorry for myself because I didn't even have a boyfriend, let alone an engagement ring.

My friends used to call me 'Generous Millie' because I was always throwing money (that I didn't have) at the bar and offering to buy everyone around me drinks. Now I'm generous with my attention, my affection and my time. Drinking made me a selfish friend, but sobriety – because of the opportunities it's given me to work on myself – has made me a more selfless, kind and considerate friend. It really is as simple as that.

While I was half right about the fact that friendship as I knew it would change for ever, I'm happy to admit that when it comes to thinking that I would struggle to connect or make new friends without alcohol, I was completely and utterly wrong. I feel it's important to point out that in sobriety you won't become best mates with everyone like before. No, you probably won't make those drunk friends in toilet queues, and there will definitely be people who you'll find it much harder to gel with.

True and authentic connections are much harder to forge in sobriety, but you'll learn to tell straight away whether you're going to get on with someone. I promise, if there's a good energy between you and you feel comfortable being yourself with them, you won't need alcohol to bond. Really, booze only helps you to make friends with people it wouldn't come naturally with, and more often than not these are the friendships that rarely withstand the test of time. They're the friendships where you say 'We must do this again soon', and then you never do.

The Initial Announcement

So how do you pluck up the courage to tell the friends you spend most of your time drinking with that you're going sober but still want to continue your friendship? How do you survive a bottom-less brunch now that you have a bottom? And how do you even begin to find people to talk to who know what you're going through?

I'll give you my best advice . . .

Be honest

I'm a fan of a cliché so here we go: honesty really is the best policy. The most common excuses people use when they want to dodge a drink are that they're on antibiotics or they're driving. The problem with using either of these get-outs is that people will always try to challenge you. If you tell them that you're on medication, they'll unreliably inform you that you can drink while taking most antibiotics these days (which is not advisable), and if you continue to disagree then they'll proceed to ask you exactly *which* antibiotics you're on and then insist on googling them to check whether you can or not.

Now, if you say that you're driving, more often than not people will forcefully insist that you leave your car at the venue. Sometimes they'll even go as far as to offer to drive you back to said venue the next morning to collect said car. In my opinion, constantly having to think up rebuttals to defend your decision not to drink can just create more stress and make you more likely to succumb to peer pressure.

Keep it honest. You don't need to add timeframes, but I find that simply saying, 'I'm actually not drinking at the moment' tends to work like a charm.

Start small

If making a public announcement about your sobriety to all your nearest and dearest at once feels both overwhelming and unnecessarily dramatic, then I suggest you disclose it to at least one friend to begin with, and recommend you start with the one you think will be the most supportive.

The reason I don't advise keeping your new alcohol-free life a complete secret is that sticking to sobriety is hard, especially in the first few months and especially if you do it alone. Entrusting your decision to at least one person will help to hold you accountable and not only will that person be someone to give you a cautioning side-eye if you even so much as sniff a G & T, but they will also be an ally – a secret-mission partner and someone who can help you execute an escape plan if you're out and things get a little too much.

Try not to leave it too long to tell your other friends. There can be a tendency to overthink this part of the process and, try as you might, you can't predict or control people's reactions, no matter how long you leave an announcement. It might turn out they don't understand, it might turn out that they couldn't care less. To be perfectly honest, you'll find it's largely the latter. Either way, it's better to work out quickly who you can rely on during this time.

Sometimes I liken telling people that you've given up drinking to getting a drastic new haircut. At first, you think everyone around you will either not recognize you and have to do a double-take or will fall off their chair in complete shock. Despite it feeling as though your world has dramatically shifted, the reality is that hardly anyone will even notice.

When something feels like a massively life-transforming change for us, we tend to magnify the anticipated reactions of others, but in reality these changes are actually pretty small to the people we're telling, and are never as important to them as they are to us.

Don't read into their reactions

I didn't understand the haircut theory when I was in early sobriety, so upon telling my friends that I was going sober I expected them to throw me a party or declare that they no longer wanted to be friends with me. I concluded that there would be banners emblazoned with congratulatory messages that dropped from the ceiling and a cannon to shoot out sparkly confetti, or there would be an immediate 'inter-friend-tion' to discuss my future within the group. None of that happened, of course. Instead, they were largely and underwhelmingly unfazed.

Looking back, it was as if I'd told them I was thinking about buying some new earrings rather than making what felt like the biggest decision of my life to date. There were a few mutters of encouragement, a couple of insinuations that I wasn't going to be fun, and several nods of agreement that it sounded like an 'interesting idea'. There wasn't a banner, balloon or look of absolute horror in sight.

The more I've thought about it, the less my friends' reactions surprise me. It's fair to say we've all been so hungover that we've vowed never to drink again. Even searching those words on my WhatsApp chat brings up eight archived conversations where I've declared it so passionately, only to have done a one-eighty by the following Friday when I've asked who's ready to 'get fucked up'.

After several chats with my friends, I now know that it wasn't that they were unsupportive, they just assumed it was another case of me talking the talk but not following through with my decision. Actions speak louder than words, and at that point my words about giving up alcohol sounded rather hollow. It was only a few months into my abstinence that they realized it was something I wasn't budging on, and it was then that they pulled out their metaphorical pom-poms and rallied behind me like a bunch of supportive cheerleaders.

For the purpose of this book I decided to ask my mates if they had ever felt angry at the decision I'd made and thankfully, true to form, they weren't any less than brutally honest. While they collectively agreed that they did in fact go through a mini-mourning process for the old me, they also agreed that once they saw how happy I was becoming – and simultaneously realized that this meant they would never have to talk me out of another toilet meltdown, or have to ask the bouncers to remove me from the club I'd refused to leave – then they were pretty relieved to lay drunk me to rest and welcome her reincarnated version.

It seems I'm not alone in this experience. When I asked around to see if anyone else's friends had a frankly disappointing reaction to their announcement of sobriety, the consensus was a pretty resounding yes. And when I asked if these reactions shifted to something more supportive over time, the feedback was also pretty positive:

'They weren't bothered when I told them because they didn't believe me.'

'They laughed it off at first and said I should still drink on special occasions.'

'They were really shocked in the beginning but now they're very proud and supportive.'

'Some thought I wasn't serious at first and laughed, but eventually everyone got on board.'

'They were really encouraging but I don't think they thought I would stick to it.'

'Now they see how I'm the same – energetic and happy just minus the drink – they're supportive.'

And most poignantly . . .

'Their attitudes have completely changed. Seeing an improvement in me has helped their understanding.'

So the moral is, if the reactions to your sober 'unveiling' are less than savoury, it's likely that they won't always stay that way, especially when your friends start to witness you magically blossoming in front of them. Better days will come, and true friends will recognize and celebrate what's best for you in the end.

Going Forward

As well as reliably informing friends about your new-found tee-totalism, the other item of business on your agenda is to establish a few ground rules and face your first major obstacle – drunk people. Here's how best to handle it . . .

Set boundaries

It can be so important to set boundaries in life. Letting people know what we are and aren't comfortable with is the key to success in so many areas of our wellbeing, and it's paramount to establish firm ones around booze. One of my boundaries is that I won't get involved in buying rounds now. Even if my mocktails are as expensive as my friends' cocktails, I don't tend to buy more than two or three (because there's only so much liquid you can tolerate in one sober sitting). So I just make it clear to count me out because I'd rather do my own thing.

More recently, another thing that I've been quite clear about is that I don't feel comfortable buying alcohol as a gift. At the start of my sobriety, I tried to compensate for my lack of drinking at gatherings like dinner parties by making sure I always bought the host a bottle of wine or the latest flavoured gin. But actually, the further I've moved along in my journey, and the greater understanding I have about what booze does to us, I've realized that I no longer consider a bottle of bubbly to be a kind and thoughtful gift.

If you don't feel comfortable ordering alcoholic drinks for your friends, going to certain bars, or even talking about why you've decided to give up drinking, then it's crucial that you tell them. Personally, there aren't many things I find too upsetting any more, and running a sober platform where I like to open up conversations around alcohol means it's kind of counter-productive for me to shut someone down when they ask why I don't drink.

Your boundaries can also vary depending on the situation, or even the person. You might be super comfortable talking to the kind stranger who asked why you gave up drinking, because they asked in such a genuinely interested and lovely way, but you might not fancy regaling your whole office with the story when your boozed-up boss is trying to out you at a staff party. It's OK to be flexible with your boundaries, so get to know what you're comfortable with in a variety of settings.

Expect a taste of your own medicine

I'm often asked how I tolerate drunk people. The answer is not very well, but the difference for me is *who* these drunk people are. If they're random people invading my personal space with beer breath and long-winded stories, I'm reluctant to entertain them. If they're my life-long friends, I've resigned myself to the fact that, for a while at least, I'll be paying them back for all the occasions when they've looked after me: the times they've held my hair back, the times they've stopped me from going home with strangers, and the times I've been an absolute cow to them. I quite like the fact that however annoying they become on a night out, I can always make sure they get home safely. The trick is to see yourself as less sober sheep-herder and more sober guardian angel.

However, this attitude doesn't mean you need to have absolute patience 100 per cent of the time, so don't be afraid to make a few things clear. After all, drunk people tend to repeat themselves, and the only thing more boring than someone telling the same story twice is having to listen to it! If this ever happens to you, I suggest you smile, put on your politest voice and just say, 'You've already told me this story.' Chances are, if they're already repeating stories, they're also at the stage when they will forget you even said anything, so be selfish and save yourself.

Here are a few more specific pointers to help you out in different social situations . . .

Nights Out

So you've told your friends you're sober and you've set your boundaries. Now it's time to get your dancing shoes on (might I recommend a comfy block heel) and head out. Here's how you can manage going 'out out' without feeling left out.

Suggest alternative activities

Nine times out of ten, we end up arranging activities that revolve around drinking because it's easy to do so. Meeting at a cocktail bar or a restaurant is convenient and doesn't require too much planning. If you really want to do things that aren't centred around alcohol, you need to pull your finger out and get organizing. Yes, it would be nice if your friends thought about this too, but ultimately they'll be happy to opt for whatever is simplest. So, for a little bit at least, it's down to you.

Disco nap

One of the differences you'll notice on a sober night out is that you'll get tired far quicker than if you were drinking. So if you plan on sticking it out until the wee hours of the morning without falling asleep on the dance floor, then a disco nap is imperative. Sometimes I take mine while everyone else is having pre-drinks and just arrive at the party a little late.

Make plans for a Saturday and not Friday

This applies as a general rule for everyone over the age of twenty-eight who finds the idea of clubbing exhausting, but even more so if you're not drinking. Friday is the night when most people finish work; it's the night when all you really want to do is go home, order a takeaway and put your pyjamas on. Trying to motivate yourself to go out and shake it until the early hours of Saturday morning is hard at best and near impossible without the prospect of booze. Make your plans for a Saturday so you'll be fresh, rested and find it much easier to get into the spirit of it all! If you work on a weekend then find another day that suits you. Sometimes it's better to make plans for week nights because there's rarely an expectation to stay out past midnight.

Take regular breaks

Being sober in a club or a bar can get a little overwhelming at times, so be sure to take regular breathers. I don't really advise heading to the smoking area, because it's unlikely you'll get much fresh air there, but even if you take well-timed bathroom breaks – just to give yourself five minutes of space when it all gets too much – you'll feel much better as a result.

Ride the wave

From personal research conducted through the Sober Girl Society, I came to realize that there was an agreement among members that the enjoyment of a sober night out is not necessarily a linear thing.

For me, the first hour is always quite a bumpy ride – it takes me a while to shake off any social awkwardness and settle into the situation. The first hour is also normally when I might struggle to find a good alcohol-free drink or the bartender says something well intended but slightly embarrassing like, 'You know that drink you've ordered is a mocktail, right?' Meanwhile, your friends are all clinking their glasses of prosecco and cackling.

After this there tends to be a good few hours when I find things much smoother sailing. I notice that I start to cruise on everyone else's relaxed vibe and I find myself loving life – maybe I'm just intoxicated from the smell of tequila. Sometimes the good vibes continue until the end and other times I end up helping my sobbing, drunk friend look for her bag. No two nights are the same, so I just kind of go with it.

An interesting thing to remember is that the booze buzz might all be in our heads. Professor Nutt explains this in his book *Drink?* by recounting details of a study in New Zealand that put people into a room that looked like a bar. Half the participants were told that they were drinking tonic and the other half were told that they were drinking vodka tonic. What the experimenters actually did was rim the 'vodka tonic' glasses with lime and dunk them in vodka so they smelled of alcohol but were totally alcohol-free. Despite not consuming any alcohol the participants in this group acted drunk, flirting and giggling. Even when told otherwise, some of them still believed that they had been drinking an alcoholic drink.

Unleashing your dancing diva

Let's be honest, unless you're an absolute pro, the prospect of moving your limbs in public without first having consumed a few drinks can be daunting. So, who better to ask for some tips on sober dancing and how to fake it until you make it than celebrity choreographer and honorary SGS member AJ O'Neill. It's worth mentioning here that AJ believes dancing should be accessible to everyone, so he offers options for dancers who use wheelchairs as well as teaching seated classes.

- ♥ Until you build up your confidence, I suggest you dance with friends who get you. It's important to feel comfortable around the people you're dancing with, so starting with your boss at the office party isn't recommended.

- ♥ Dance to the right song – a killer tune does 90 per cent of the work, after all. Sober dancing is the same as sober anything: if it's not fun, it's not because you're not drunk, it's because you aren't feeling it. Music you love is what makes it fun.

- ♥ Can you dance in your bedroom when no one's watching? Then you can dance anywhere. If you feel you've lost the ability to dance sober, dance round your house first!

♥ Look at everyone else dancing. Realize how daft they look and how little you judge them for it. Then apply that same logic to any self-consciousness that's holding you back. Have a sense of humour about it. Dancing is silly, life is silly. Dance like someone who gets how silly life is.

♥ Wear something you're comfortable dancing in. If you're worried about toppling over in your six-inch heels, it'll make it virtually impossible for you to relax and really get into the swing of things.

♥ Take classes. If sober dancing is beyond terrifying for you, try to learn a few basic moves that might give you some added confidence on the dance floor. There's literally a million different dance styles, so take time to find something you enjoy.

♥ Less is more. You don't have to be able to do the lift from *Dirty Dancing* (no one can really do the lift from *Dirty Dancing*), but just finding the beat and moving your hips to the rhythm is enough. Remember, you're dancing for yourself and no one else.

Get your alcohol-free drink on!

Nights out are always better if you get to drink something you like. From experience, Diet Coke is great but beware: the amount of caffeine in six Diet Cokes will give you heart palpitations. Choose venues that have a good selection of alcohol-free options, and if you need help navigating a menu, then Chapter Nine will give you all the tips you need to become a beverage connoisseur!

Curate your own show

Sometimes I like to imagine myself having a kind of out-of-body experience where I just observe everyone around me, as if I'm not really there and I'm just watching them on the television, like an episode of *Gogglebox*. In her book *The Unexpected Joy of Being Sober*, Catherine Gray likens this to assuming the persona of David Attenborough and studying the strange behavioural patterns and mating rituals of the wildlife around you in their natural habitat. But on a serious note, stepping out of the situation and seeing myself as an outsider can really calm me down and help me not to get swept up in all the craziness.

Sortie française

Last but not least, my final resort would be to suggest the old French exit. If you really don't feel like sticking it out to the end of the night, and think your sobriety or sanity could be compromised if you were to stay any longer, then slip away quietly. The harsh truth is that most people will be too drunk to notice you've left, but make sure you drop people a quick text to let them know you haven't been abducted.

Bottomless Brunches

Over the last five years, the unlimited midday piss-up has become a gal-pal staple, and navigating an event where the whole point is to get as sloshed as possible in a designated amount of time certainly takes some willpower. Here's my tried-and-tested advice to help you make it out alive.

Make sure there's a boozeless option

Call ahead, email, stalk the restaurant on Instagram. Do whatever it takes to make sure you have something to drink other than water. If you need to, go ahead, pull out the pregnancy card and ask if you can bring your own – there's no judgement here. And remember to respect your boundaries.

Don't drink too much of said boozeless option

This might sound strange, but believe me when I say that seven mocktails will make you feel fairly queasy and give you a sugar headache to rival any hangover. Don't try to keep up with the pace of those who are drinking. I've legitimately been very ill after bottomless alcohol-free Mimosas, because I don't think any human is supposed to consume that amount of juice in one go. And trust me: if you're not drunk, you'll really feel the effects.

Focus on the brunch part

In case you need reminding, it's brunch! As someone who has frequently seen their brunch reappear in reverse order, I can tell you that the food is often overshadowed at this kind of event. We all know it's mainly there to cushion the blow of drinking (aka lining the stomach) but not for you! Go to town and order several courses: eggs three different ways, a variety of sides . . . Treating myself to make up for the lack of booze is key for me, and extra items from the menu is one of my favourite ways to do that!

Make post-brunch plans

We all know the score: whoever planned the boozy brunch dreamed big and imagined that everyone would carry on throughout the day before heading to a club in the evening . . . In reality, every bottomless brunch I've been to has ended abruptly after someone's thrown up in a Bellini jug, so I recommend always having a back-up plan you can turn to if things descend into carnage. If by some miracle the party does continue, you might also want to use your other plans as an excuse to leave.

Dinner and House Parties

Both these events can feel tricky to navigate, and whether you're attending or hosting, there's a lot you can do to take the focus off you not drinking. And yes, a lot of it involves organized fun.

Bring the mixers

There are some pretty fancy tonics out there these days – from Double Dutch's pomegranate and basil to Merchant Heart's pink peppercorn – that will impress your guests as much as a boozy beverage, so offer to bring the mixers (or supply them if you're hosting). That way, you can add an alcohol-free spirit to yours and your guests can add their own alcohol if they wish. If you're hosting, don't be afraid to implement a BYOB rule and explain that you'll provide absolutely everything else.

Orchestrate the entertainment

If you're hosting the dinner party, be sure to organize some fun activities. From personal experience, I find that if the party's feeling a little flat in the absence of booze they can be just what's needed. Entertainment doesn't need to be extravagant – please don't go forking out for Michael Bublé to serenade your guests – an easy game such as Articulate can get the party going.

If you're attending, offer to be the one to bring the entertainment. Your role as quiz/games host will not only give you something to do that isn't drinking, but it will also automatically score you some 'fun points' and force you out of your shell. If you manage to get people having a good time, they'll forget you're not even drinking.

Learn the perfect pairings

Did you know there are actual water sommeliers who can detect complex properties in different glasses of H_2O? Yep. Although you might not want to go that far, doing some basic research into how to pair non-alcoholic drinks with your meal can really elevate the dining experience for you or your guests!

Toby Amphlett is a national ambassador for Æcorn, an aperitif brand part of the Seedlip family. Toby believes that a simple way to pair is to break down the flavours of the dish you're eating and link them to the structure of the drink. For example, the Æcorn 'Bitter' variety is bold and complex, with influences of citrus. Therefore, Toby recommends thinking high-fat/salt-content foods such as cured, grilled, sweet starches or anything dairy-influenced. He says it's great with tapas or antipasti-style dishes.

Be the DJ

Nothing sets the tone of a party as much as its backing track, so if you're hosting make sure you have a killer playlist ready. Ask your guests for suggestions of what they'd like to listen to on the night and watch how excited they get when they hear their song.

Hen Parties

When I asked on Instagram which social events with friends you found it hardest not to drink at, it was no surprise that hen parties came out on top. I'm not sure if that's down to their raucous reputation or the fact that quite often you're mixing with people you've never met before (like the bride's cousin's girlfriend). As someone who's experienced their fair share of hen parties sober – and even one where we made a trip to the local gin distillery – I can whole-heartedly agree that they can be difficult to master.

While it isn't my preferred option, not attending is always a possibility. So if you're feeling really uncomfortable, offer to take your friend out separately instead. Failing that, find out if not staying over or even having your own room are viable options to make the whole thing less full-on. Should you choose to feel the fear and do it anyway, here's my advice to help you through.

Offer to be the challenge initiator

If you've ever been on a hen, you'll know that the bride usually has to take part in a set of challenges, which can range from swapping clothes with a stranger, to kissing a bald man on the head – or perhaps that's just the ones I've been on! Either way, offering to be the one to lead the charge is always appreciated (not necessarily by the bride), especially if you feel a little on the outside because you're not legless by 3 p.m. It's a great way to keep yourself involved.

Look for the similarities not the differences

It's easy to presume that the only common ground you'll have with someone is that you both like to get wasted, but it's simply not the case. If you're on a hen with people you don't know, then try to find out if you have other shared interests. Knowing the bride is something you both have in common (otherwise you wouldn't be there) so that's always a good place to start.

Do your own shots

I came across this tip on the *Huffington Post* about doing a sober stag do.[1] While I don't really agree with it, I think it could be worth noting for some of the more hardcore amongst us. The idea is that a lot of the bonding that goes on during these weekends (and, indeed, through drinking together in general) is thanks to collective suffering – a kind of 'we're all in this together' mentality.

You should *never* do anything you don't feel comfortable with. Nor should you do anything because you want to prove something, or because you want people to like you. But if you're kind of wild and want to get your kicks, writer Ruari recommends downing a shot of lime cordial (it's really gross on its own) to show that you too can suffer along with the group – just without booze.[2]

Have the conversations

Let me tell you now that, as the sober one, at some point on a hen do you will be quietly cornered and quizzed about your choice. The truth is, whether they want to admit it or not, everyone wants a little holiday from booze and you'll be the shining, alcohol-free lighthouse that everyone will gravitate to when they're feeling like they might have had enough. You may start the weekend as 'the sensible one', but when the hangovers appear you'll end the weekend as the one everyone wishes they'd been from the start.

Document it

Hen weekends are about the bride, and it's more than likely that she and everyone else will be too hammered to remember to take nice photos for the memory bank. Position yourself as the paparazzi and capture all the best moments – everyone will thank you afterwards (depending on the evidence!).

Weddings

Despite the fact that weddings are supposed to be the happiest day of some people's lives, if it's not yours and you have to do it sober, you can begin to think that quite the opposite is true. There are two main reasons why weddings are notoriously difficult to navigate without a drink.

The first is that nuptials are a kind of 'all-in' package deal. With some other social events, you can simply leave if you're feeling horrifically bored or out of sorts. However, at a wedding it's much harder to stand up during your second course, or in the middle of the best man's speech, and declare that you've actually just had enough. There's a certain level of expectation as a wedding guest that you're more or less locked in for the duration, and that duration is often rather lengthy.

The second is the more obvious reason – it's difficult to avoid the free-flowing booze. From the prosecco during the toasts to the abundance of wine with every course, trying to keep turning down drinks when they're literally being forced into your hand can be tricky, even for the most seasoned sober pro. Try these tips to make sure you stick to your sober commitment.

Know that your presence is a present

It's worth acknowledging that the most wonderful gift you can give a happy couple on their big day is to be fully present in the moment. Weddings are supposed to be the ultimate celebration of human connection, yet everyone tends to become so intoxicated that this sentiment often seems to get lost. Being sober at a wedding means that you're honouring what the ceremony is really about, and you'll get to witness every moment of pure joy between the couple.

Remember, months – or even years – of planning has gone into the day, so being sober means you'll notice and appreciate all the effort made and the details (from chair bows to table decorations) that the pair have scrupulously debated.

Ego-check yourself

It helps to remind yourself that the day is not about you, so don't begrudge the newlyweds if they haven't had the forethought to provide a selection of interesting drinks for sober guests. They'll have enough on their plate in the lead-up to the event, so tell them you don't mind calling the venue yourself. If you find out that there's not much on offer, see if they'll let you bring along something of your own.

Lend a hand

Ask the couple if you can help with anything on the day, especially if you're close to them. It's a stressful time for the wedding party, so not only will they likely be grateful for an extra pair of hands, but having something to do can also help you feel less anxious. Even if it's just helping to move the cake from one table to another.

Be the babysitter

Offer to spend some time looking after any children attending the wedding. Your mum mates will appreciate an hour off and your hands will be too full to even think about holding a drink. Best of all, kids (almost) never question why you aren't drinking!

Enlist back-up

Find a sober supporter. Whether that's your date, a pregnant friend or someone at the end of a WhatsApp message who gets what a challenge it can be and will pep-talk you through a wobble, it helps to know there's someone looking out for you.

Use some of your night-out tools

Curate your own show, dance like no one is watching and take regular breaks – all the same tactics apply at weddings. In some ways they're even more relevant here because you have to get through the day *and* night.

Get ready to gloat!

Without booze to hamper my reflexes and my hand–eye coordination, I'm often the most likely candidate to catch the bouquet at any wedding. Make sure to stretch first, though – if you pull a muscle you'll be sure to feel it more than if you were drunk.

Your Soberversary

A very little-known perk of sobriety is that you get to add a whole new celebration to the calendar – your sober anniversary! If your friends are kind enough to humour you, it's a great day to organize an alcohol-free activity. You could invite the girls round for a pyjama party or mocktail-making session. Chances are your mates won't be as excited about the actual reason for the celebration as you are, but it's still a fun excuse for you all to get together.

Feeling Like a Hypocrite

If you'd have told anyone who knew me five years ago that I would be writing a book about sobriety, they would have laughed in your face. Luckily – or unluckily – Facebook memories does a pretty good job of reminding me of how far I've come on my sobriety journey. Photos regularly pop up of me wearing one shoe and smeared lipstick, with a caption along the lines of having lost my phone once again.

After years of pushing people to do tequila shots and encouraging them to drink faster, feeling like I would be a complete hypocrite for suddenly declaring that I was teetotal was just one of the many reasons I didn't give up alcohol sooner. Something I wish I'd realized is that we all have the right (providing we aren't hurting anyone) to reinvent ourselves as whoever or whatever we want to be, whenever we choose. You're allowed to have a light-bulb moment and you're allowed to do a one-eighty on everything you thought you believed.

I can't promise that no one will ever call you out for being a hypocrite in sobriety. The only thing you can do in that situation is to explain that you no longer want to be the person that you once were, and that you're trying to be a better one. You can even quote one of my favourite philosophers, Rachel Greene from *Friends*: 'It's like all of my life everyone has always told me, "You're a shoe. You're a shoe, you're a shoe, you're a shoe." And then today I just stopped and I said, "What if I don't want to be a shoe? What if I want to be a purse, you know, or a hat?"'

Be that hat.

Re-evaluating Friendships

If you get a few months down the sobriety line and find that those around you are still being unsupportive, it could be time to seriously reflect on whether you want these people in your life. It might sound like an extreme reaction, and it can certainly be a tough lesson to learn, but people who don't support your sobriety ultimately don't support you.

When I asked SGS followers if they'd lost any friends through becoming sober, there were certainly a few who had. If you find you do, don't be disheartened. You are not alone!

> *'Yes, we didn't have anything in common apart from alcohol and I've grown up.'*
>
> *'I lost one friend, but she was toxic for me and I never realized until I lost booze from our dynamic.'*
>
> *'Yes, if our only mutual interest was alcohol then I've drifted away.'*
>
> *'Yes, because I realized we only connected when drinking and that's not true friendship.'*

Before you go cutting people out left, right and centre, however, let them know how you feel. It might be that an honest conversation needs to be had. Maybe they think you've got a bit preachy about the benefits of your new-found sobriety. Maybe you've made people question their own relationship with drinking and they don't like it and so become defensive. Maybe it is – like a lot of the girls quoted above found out – that you've both simply realized that booze is the glue that's been holding you together, and without it you don't actually have much in common. Whatever the reason, if you can't work through it, it might be time to let that friend-ship sail!

Ask for help

If you're sober curious, beginning your sober journey, or still a little hesitant about telling your friends how you're feeling – I've got you. I know that sometimes those conversations can be hard, so here's a list you can highlight, underline, bookmark or screenshot to let people know how they can best support you. What follows are the things I wanted my friends to know when I first gave up drinking:

- Our friendship is really important to me and I feel I'm a better friend sober.

- Please don't assume that I don't want to come to things now – I definitely do.

- If I turn one thing down, it might be because it feels daunting right now. Don't think that means I'll turn everything down in the future.

- It's disheartening when you suggest that I'm boring – I'm still fun, I promise.

- Please don't think I judge you for still drinking – I absolutely don't!

- I'd love it if you took me into consideration when throwing a dinner party, in the same way you'd cater to a vegan. It's awesome when you feel like someone's thought about you.

♥ Understand that I might want to leave events early. This doesn't mean I haven't had fun, I'm just ready to go home.

♥ Please assist in my voice being heard. When everyone gets drunk and shouty, I may go quiet. It's not because I have nothing to say but sometimes lots of voices can be overwhelming.

♥ I'd love it if you offered to do sober things with me. I don't mind spending my time in bars, but I'd really appreciate it if we could mix things up a bit.

♥ Please think about me when it comes to splitting the bill. I don't mind if you've had a couple of glasses of wine, but when it turns into bottles I'd like to just pay for myself!

Finding New Friends

When I started Sober Girl Society, the aim was to connect people through shared experiences. I imagined I would follow a few people, stalk them from afar, and maybe swap a few messages at best. I assumed we'd talk about the best sober quotes or compare exchanges we'd had with grumpy bar staff, but I didn't really think it would go much deeper than that.

Despite their initial ambivalence, my existing friends had turned into my biggest sober supporters, and I assumed that other sober people would probably be boring. How's that for ironic! What I didn't realize is that by starting the society, I was launching myself into a community of the friendliest, funniest and wildest people alive.

Naturally, I've come to make sober friends through running SGS meet-ups, attending brand events and speaking on panels, and I truly never realized how invaluable they would be. I wouldn't have come so far on my journey without them. Whether it's swapping horror stories with a shared sense of (dark) humour or pep-talking each other through different stages, pitfalls and sticky situations, having people who remind me why I don't drink has been the lifeline I never knew I needed.

We're led to believe that we need to make alcohol work in our lives, be that counting our units or not mixing certain drinks. We're never really taught that there's the option to just take it off the table altogether if it's no longer serving us. Society in general loves to declare that people can't 'handle' their drink, putting the blame firmly on the drinker and not the poisonous substance. Not being able to handle something suggests that you've struggled and failed to control it successfully, and having other people around me who are making the same decision constantly re-assures me that I'm not a failure for simply removing alcohol from my life.

As well as providing extra support on top of your existing network, creating sober connections might be key if you have to re-evaluate your existing friendships. Although making friends later in life can feel a bit like putting yourself out there on your first day of school, trust me when I say there are plenty of people in the same boat and making friends might be easier than you think.

Obviously, the online sober community is a great and easily accessible place to start – friends at your fingertips! When it comes to offline, meet-ups and events are everywhere, from sober running clubs to morning raves. You can literally pitch up at anything you fancy and be welcomed with open arms. Attending just a few meet-ups a year can massively strengthen your sober resolve, even if it's just to vent to people who get it.

Here are some suggestions to get you started and there are plenty more ideas in the support and resources section (see pages 279–289).

Attend sober events

There's now a plethora of booze-free bashes running up and down the country, and they're a great way to meet people. A simple scan through Eventbrite will usually point you in the right direction, but there are also platforms such as Dice and Facebook events. Below are some of my favourites, but once you start digging around in the support and resources section, you'll find other people and places who offer them too.

Morning Gloryville: The original morning rave that offers inspiring music, mesmerizing visual entertainment, free massages, organic smoothie bars and yoga! It's completely bonkers but what's not to love?

Day Breaker: This female-owned business is the morning dance party that will set you up for your day with energy and intention. You can catch it across the world from LA to London, Mexico City to Miami, and Berlin to Buenos Aires.

Sober & Social: From bar crawls around the hottest nightlife spots to parties in the most exclusive clubs, Sober & Social's events have become notorious among healthy hedonists who still like to party until the early hours with style but not substance. They also host tamer events such as sharing circles for those who like to live a quieter life and a membership service for those seeking extra support.

Sober Girl Spotlight

'Sobriety has actually made me more sociable!'

Host of the Sober Sips podcast, Emily Syphas (@iamemilysyphas), stopped drinking after years of alcohol negatively impacting her work, friendships and relationships: 'From the age of twenty-five to twenty-eight, I was in this destructive cycle of drinking then not drinking before I finally decided enough was enough.'

At the time, Emily's job title was, ironically, Head of Nightlife for one of the world's largest luxury concierge services. She was still spending most of her early sobriety in clubs and bars, which quickly prompted her to recognize the lack of inclusive social spaces catering to those trying to quit or cut down on their drinking.

Following her revelation, Emily founded Sober & Social (@soberandsocial_), a community that aims to empower people to feel comfortable and confident socializing without booze. Since then, Emily has encouraged hundreds of people to face their fears about sober socializing, and is continually striving to erase the stigma of not drinking by working closely with bars and nightclubs in an effort to encourage them to accommodate this new conscious community. She also believes her own social life is better than it ever was:

> It's honestly improved tenfold since not drinking, and I enjoy social situations so much more. I'm able to enjoy the music, be present and remember everything in the morning. I'm so glad I can lead a life with confidence, clarity and conviction without alcohol. Be kind to yourself – sobriety is a journey not a destination. Find a sober community and make friends to give you support, love and accountability.

Explore Sober Communities

There really is something for everyone online, whether it's a local group that meets up and makes ceramics, or an organization with branches in every town. If you're not sure where to start, try these . . .

Sober Girl Society: If you don't already follow SGS on Instagram, then hop on over and come say hello! We run monthly events up and down the country, from bottomless boozeless brunches to our sparkly, sober sweat dance classes. You can sign up to our mailing list to see when we're in a city near you.

Club Soda: Club Soda are the pioneers when it comes to sober events. Among many other things, Laura Willoughby and her team organize the twice-yearly Mindful Drinking Festival, a free event open to anyone to come and try the latest and best alcohol-free drinks on the market. There are mocktail masterclasses and talks from motivational speakers, including yours truly. The Club Soda Facebook groups provide incredible support for everyone, whether they're cutting down, drinking mindfully or quitting the booze altogether.

AA: Despite some of the mixed press it's had in recent years, I know lots of people, such as my friend Becky, who have made lasting connections with the people they meet through the programme. AA is, of course, free, and the community aspect is at its core. There's also bound to be a meeting in your area, so you shouldn't need to travel far to find it.

Regional communities: Over the last couple of years, local sober collectives have been popping up thick and fast on Instagram, making it easier than ever to find people who live within a reasonable distance of you. A great way to discover them is to simply google the word 'sober' followed by your city, or try searching for them as a combined hashtag on social media – for example, #soberlondon or #sobermanchester. Amongst these fab UK regional groups are Sober Circle (@sober_circle) in Bristol and the South West and Sober Buzz (@soberbuzzscotland) in, you guessed it, Scotland.

If you're not on social media then meetup.com is a great place to find local sober pals. The Sober South in Cork, Ireland has nearly 3,000 members.

At SGS, we also run monthly 'Find Your Sober Sisters' threads on our Instagram page, where you can comment your global location and hook up with other women ditching the drink in your neighbourhood.

LGBTQIA+ communities: Luckily, there are wonderful communities representing queer voices in this space too. Queers Without Beers (@qwb_uk) is an online community hosting monthly events in central London, Manchester and Bristol. Everyone is welcome – whether you've never had a drink, just don't want alcohol on that night, are looking to change your drinking habits, or have actively quit drinking. Proud and Sober (@proudandsober) aims to promote sobriety in queer spaces and ensure that an alcohol-free lifestyle is celebrated in style.

BIPOC communities: For too long, the sober space on Instagram has been dominated by white voices, and it's important to understand that trauma experienced from racism can add another complex layer to the struggle of trying to get sober. Thankfully, we now have communities like @soberbrowngirls, @servedupsober and @soberblackgirlsclub.

Make connections

What might feel like creepy behaviour in most situations is almost encouraged in the alcohol-free community. If you find individuals you want to connect with, reach out to them. I made one of my very best sober friends when he messaged me for advice and we found out that our offices in London were within touching distance. We went for a mocktail in a very classy establishment (All Bar One) and now we know each other's darkest secrets – so this kind of friendship can escalate pretty quickly!

Try the apps

There are a few apps out there for making sober friends, but they're primarily based in the US. For the UK I recommend Bumble – you might be surprised to find that no, it's not just a dating app! The friend section of Bumble (Bumble BFF) enables you to find local friends in your area and there's also a filter that allows you to discover people who don't drink too.

Start something yourself

I started the Sober Girl Society because I believed there wasn't anything out there like it. If you feel like your country, city or town needs an alcohol-free community, you could create one. It's a lot of work but it's so worth it, and you might end up making life-long friends.

Lastly, a Few Things to Keep in Mind . . .

If you ever meet up with strangers on the internet, the usual safety rules apply – stick to public places and let others know where you are. As a final thought, please don't be disheartened if you don't immediately click with other sober people. I don't believe two sober people will instantly become best friends in the same way that I don't believe two single people will instantly fall in love just because they're both unattached. However, I will point out that I have yet to meet a sober person I haven't liked, or at least been able to hold a decent conversation with, and I think that's down to the fact that anyone questioning their relationship with alcohol is simply wanting to become a better version of themselves, and people who want to do that are my kind of people.

Sober Girl Gains

☐ Memories you will actually remember

☐ Being able to show up for your friends

☐ Knowing you'll never drunkenly ruin a mate's birthday/ wedding/baby shower

☐ Brand-new, shiny, sparkly sober pals

☐ A new date for your diary – your soberversary!

7

Young Hearts, Rum-free

Romantic relationships and drink-free dating

Like most girls my age, I was brought up on a steady stream of Disney princesses and Ross and Rachel-esque endings which, for a long time, led me to believe that my life wouldn't officially begin until I'd either been rescued by my Prince Charming or got off the plane.

When I was nineteen I met a boy in Ayia Napa. He lived in Birmingham and I was at university in Brighton, but with a little help from National Express we made it work. For six years he was the Ross to my Rachel, until he wasn't.

When we broke up, I plunged into a revolving state of ragey outbursts and self-pity. I felt abandoned, hurt, and spent every minute of every day wondering what was so fundamentally wrong with me that I wasn't worthy of love. The only time I wasn't staring at my face debating what enhancing surgery I could get, or wondering if he'd still be there if I'd worn sexier underwear, was when I was either asleep or drunk.

Craving validation and confirmation that I wasn't completely unlovable, I threw myself into online dating. In my mind, even if I didn't like whoever sat opposite me, meeting up with strangers off the internet was another perfectly reasonable excuse to get shit-faced and avoid untangling the mess of emotions that raged inside me like a washing machine on the verge of packing up.

Unsurprisingly, booze heightened most things for me, and matters of the heart were definitely no exception. Because I was so desperate not to feel sad, drinking made that desperation sort of bubble over and manifest itself as me clinging on to anything with a pulse and a penis. I started to emerge from pretty much all of my drunken dates with instructions to my friends and family to go out immediately and buy a hat for my impending nuptials, because I'd found The One.

It was a good job they didn't start buying fascinators willy-nilly because most of those dates either ghosted me or I'd meet them the following week and swiftly realize that the only thing we really had in common was that we were both very heavy drinkers. It's amazing how gin can create a spark from literally nothing.

I'm aware that in the wider context of life there are much more painful things to experience than heartbreak, and looking back now I am mildly embarrassed to have given it so much weight. But for anyone who has ever experienced romantic loss, you will know that when you are in it, nothing feels like it could be worse.

The sparkly world of swiping lost its appeal quickly, and I settled on the fact that drunken nights out and quick hook-ups were a far more efficient way to heal my heartbreak. Ironically, most nights I was far too hammered to attempt to pull anyone, but the times that I did, my memory was often hazy and lines of consent started to become dangerously blurry.

As trips to the sexual health clinic became more frequent, respect for my own body and boundaries became quite the opposite. I felt vast and empty, and alcohol was the only thing that seemed to inject some of the life – which I no longer felt – back into me. Alcohol gave me a personality, albeit a shitty one, when all I really felt was dark and lost. It became my flimsy coat of armour that was holding the remaining fragments of me together and upright, protecting what was underneath. But it was never the solution.

If anything, it was just the cause of more problems. If I wasn't partying then I was hungover, anxious and crying – stuck in a hamster wheel of misery and self-sabotage that I knew couldn't continue any longer. I was so tired of being sad, I was so tired of the shame I felt from the things I was doing, and I was so tired of throwing pity parties for one because a boy had broken my heart.

Reading parts of *The Unexpected Joy of Being Sober* actually made me angry. Not blue-in-the-face angry, but fire-in-the-belly angry because it made me realize that the only person who was really hurting me was me. Someone had essentially told me that they didn't think I was good enough and there I was, proving them right by sabotaging my own body and mind. I realized that I could either continue on my spiral of doom, gloom and Jäger-bombs or dig deep, pull myself out of the mess I'd made and start living a life that I had always dreamed of.

For the first couple of months of my sobriety I played the sober-dating game pretty safely. I went on a date with someone I already knew, and I went out with boys that I'd already met on nights out so that I knew an initial attraction was there. None of them worked out, but they were a great place to start, and being sober meant that I could be rational about all of them.

I never got ahead of myself and I didn't tell anyone to order a hat. More importantly, with a new level of heightened self-respect, my desperation morphed into a kind of chilled indifference, knowing that it wasn't a race to find my other half because I was already becoming a full person on my own.

Once I'd built up a little confidence, I cast my net wider, and sober dating became easier and more fun than I'd ever imagined. Of course it was different, with a little more apprehension and worry involved, but every date taught me something. Eventually, I learned a lot. I learned that most people didn't see my sobriety as a deal-breaker, that clear-headed sexual chemistry is more intense than an intoxicated fumble, and that I could trust my intuition without booze clouding it.

I think booze interfered with my ability to trust my own gut instinct for a long time. Once you know that alcohol can disrupt the balance of your gut microbiota, it doesn't seem all that surprising.

When I learned to trust myself again, some of the biggest changes happened. Sobriety gave me the time to work on myself. I took up paddle boarding, started going to the gym, read self-help books, watched documentaries about the world, and reconnected with things that I loved before drinking became my go-to for happiness. I started to find new things that I liked or didn't like, and I started to work out who I really was.

This conversation has a wider scope than just dating, but when I gave up alcohol I realized that I didn't know who I was without it. For the last however many years, my identity had been inextricably caught up with drinking. Every meme I got tagged in was booze-themed, every present I was given I could drink. A lot of early sobriety was spent realizing who Millie really was.

I found out pretty quickly that I wasn't as extroverted as I thought I was, that I liked 10 a.m. more than 10 p.m., that outer space fascinated me, and that eighties music is my absolute favourite. Here's the best bit – I actually started to like Millie a little bit! I finally stopped seeking approval by trying to embody what I thought people wanted me to be and focused on who I wanted to be.

Because of this I found that I had loads more to discuss on dates than just the places I partied. I never went into a date worrying what we would talk about, because I knew that I had a list of interests as long as my arm. I was becoming the best possible version of myself and decided that I would only fall head over heels for someone who was doing the same. I would set my standards high, not in terms of a picky list of must-haves, but in seeking someone who believed in me as much as I believed in myself; someone who saw me for who I really am.

Something very strange starts to happen when you like yourself – or, at the very least, have respect for yourself – and that is that other people start to like and respect you too. Potential partners responded positively to the fact that I was confident enough in myself to do a date sober. They liked that I knew who I was and they liked that I had made a choice to put myself first rather than caring about what someone else might think about my not drinking.

There are potential pitfalls, of course, one being that sometimes people thought I might judge them for drinking. At which point I'd have to explain that the most important thing for me was that they respected my sobriety versus actually having to be sober themselves. Another hazard being that sober sexual encounters become a whole different ballgame (no pun intended), requiring all the new-found self-confidence you can muster.

That aside, with all the work and energy I was putting into myself, everything gradually started to fall into place for me. I got my happy ending because finally someone saved me. PLOT TWIST: that someone was me.

This is one of the biggest things I've learned through sobriety – I am my own Prince Charming. My life was never going to begin once I'd found someone to love me, because that would mean I was defining my worth by someone else's opinion of me. Sobriety has allowed me to trust myself, respect myself and love myself, and that's a good enough happy ending for me.

Before we get too carried away – despite all the wonderful perks, I need to acknowledge that sober dating is still terrifying, so here are a few practical tips I've picked up for sober swiping and beyond.

Dating

Even if you're drinking, dating can be one of the most nerve-racking experiences on the planet, but there are a few things you can do to make the whole thing a little more pain-free and, dare I say it . . . enjoyable!

Use the tools available

A few of the major dating apps – Bumble and Hinge included – have jumped on the sober train and introduced handy features to make the whole process a little smoother and, frankly, less daunting than it already is. You can now choose to stipulate on your profile that you don't drink, eliminating any pressure of it becoming the first topic of conversation and, if you're curious to date someone else with an alcohol-free lifestyle, you can filter your choices down to people who are sober too.

Be upfront

You don't owe your date the details of your drinking habits, but telling them ahead of time that you don't drink can avoid any pre-date panic about how they might react if you tell them in person. This allows you to concentrate on a killer outfit and to go into the date as relaxed as possible.

Prepare yourself for rejection

Some people won't be on board with your sobriety for whatever reason. Usually it's something ridiculous and will say a lot more about them than it does about you, so learn to laugh about this. Catherine Gray says that telling a potential suitor that you're sober is a fantastic dickhead detector, and honestly, I've never heard anything more accurate.

Learn new ways to settle pre-date nerves

When Dutch courage is no longer an option, you need to find new ways to overcome first-date jitters. Try a quick meditation or go to the gym beforehand to release any nervous energy. If you opt for the exercise route, remember to shower before the date.

People shouldn't judge you for your sobriety but they will judge you if you're super sweaty!

Other options include curating what I like to call a 'sass play-list', or meeting a sympathetic mate beforehand for a pre-date pep-talk.

Set your boundaries (get used to doing this!)

I'm often asked if I find it difficult to be on a date with someone who is drinking while I'm sober, but rarely has anyone been shit-faced in my company one-to-one. You'll probably find, as I have, that people don't really feel the need to drink as much when you aren't. Some dates have even expressed relief that their meeting with a stranger won't lead to the following day being a complete hangover-induced write-off.

If you do end up on a date with someone who is on a level of intoxication that you can't get on board with, someone who tries to encourage you to drink when you don't want to, or someone who shows an obvious lack of respect for your boundaries around alcohol – leave. From a practical perspective, having 'plans' after the date means you have an excuse to get out of there, and you can always own up to your possible escape intentions if the date is going well.

Don't concentrate on your sober status

Yes, you're sober, but you're also a wonderful human being with a million and one other attributes that make you interesting and unique. For starters, you're brave, curious and a bit of a rebel for going against societal norms, so it should be obvious to the lucky man or woman getting the pleasure of your company that you're a special babe – who should not be messed with. Don't let your sobriety define who you are, or allow it to be the focus of the date, in the same way that being a non-smoker wouldn't even be a point of discussion.

Be tolerant

Inevitably, some people will want to ask you a lot of questions about your sobriety. For me this is never a problem unless it starts to dominate the conversation, and therefore the date. I like talking about why I don't drink, because I see it as an opportunity to educate and change perceptions. At least if the date is a disaster, I feel like I've (hopefully) given them something to think about.

If you aren't comfortable talking about your sobriety then make it clear from the outset, but try not to get too frustrated. Generally, people will ask you because they're interested rather than because they're trying to offend you. Likewise, when your date asks you if you'd prefer a water or Diet Coke, try not to roll your eyes at their lack of imagination. Most people aren't aware of the growing number of choices out there, such as alcohol-free beers, wines and even spirits. For future reference, mine's an alcohol-free gin and tonic!

Location, location, location

Comfort zones aren't always a bad thing, so if you're particularly nervous about a meet-up then choose somewhere familiar that you know carries a good alcohol-free selection. Similarly, if you're new to the dating scene, the thought of sitting opposite someone as they relentlessly question you like a guest on *Piers Morgan's Life Stories* might feel overwhelming, so consider suggesting an activity that's a little more interactive. Thanks to sober dating, I am now semi-professional at mini-golf, paddle boarding and electronic darts, so there's also the lure that you might discover a hidden talent or learn a new skill.

The timing of your date can also help: day dates are great, as not only do they typically take the idea of drinking off the table, but you also get to see your date in natural lighting, which is never a bad thing early doors.

Dress to impress yourself

Pick an outfit that you're comfortable in. During my drunk-dating phase, I wore ridiculously low-cut tops and relied on the fact that a glass of wine would quieten my reservations about leaning too far forward and dropping a boob into my pasta. You don't want to spend your whole date feeling self-conscious, so dress for you in whatever makes you feel good. That said, if you're more comfortable in cleavage-flashing blouses – girl, you rock them. To me, jeans and a nice top is always a winner.

Enjoy the endgame

Not only will you wake up from 99 per cent of your dates free from embarrassment and regret, but if your selected suitor does want to see you again (and you want to see them, of course), then you'll know for sure that they are not just enamoured by the fun, carefree party girl façade that you have carefully projected. You will know that they like the real you, the honest you, the vulnerable you and – this one is key – the authentic you. That, as well as being an instant confidence booster, is pretty fucking special.

Sober Girl Spotlight

'Sobriety has actually made dating easier!'

For a number of years, operations finance manager Megan Montague (@delightsofmylife) had been using alcohol to self-medicate, until she reached a point where she was totally fed up with always feeling awful: 'There were no positives to having alcohol in my life and it was just making me miserable. Initially, I did a ninety-day no-drinking challenge, which soon became a complete life-change.'

Since getting sober, Megan's approach to dating has become totally different.

Before, I would bounce from person to person or date to date without really considering if someone was going to be genuinely good for me. I would chase the feeling of attachment, disregarding red flags, and I put up with being treated badly. These days, I really take my time to find out about a person, to discover if we are truly compatible. Red flags are no longer ignored and I don't get lost in the fantasy of a situation.

For Megan, sober dating gives her the opportunity to be herself, and not herself three cocktails in. She believes that you're more likely to meet the right person when you're being authentic and without clouded judgement. 'You also waste a lot less time with people and situations that aren't right for you, freeing up time for the right people and, more importantly – more time for you!'

Megan settles pre-date nerves by entering into the right frame of mind with music while getting ready. She plans her outfit way in advance so she's not last-minute stressing, and thinks deep breathing is a total winner for soothing your nervous system.

Relationships

Whether it's for better or worse, your romantic relationships are likely to change when you stop drinking, especially if you're used to routinely getting completely sloshed with your significant other. Here are a few things that you should prepare for.

Fewer arguments

A quick poll to ask my friends and followers if they'd ever had a drunken argument with their significant other confirmed what many already know: out of the 354 people who kindly responded, 327 said yes, they had. Later on, I asked if they thought they were more likely to have an argument with their significant other if they'd been drinking: of the 387 who answered that question, 342 also said yes. This proved my hunch, and suggests that sobriety really could be the secret to a less confrontational relationship.

Just to be sure, I reached out to Cate Campbell, BACP-accredited sex, relationships and trauma therapist, to find out if many of her coupled clients mention booze as a problem in their partnership. 'About 40 per cent cite it as a serious problem and about 80 per cent of those who drink say it doesn't help,' she told me.

In fact, when working on communication skills and problem resolution as part of the therapeutic process, Cate requests that clients don't drink before or during exercises she sets, nor around important conversations, because all communication is more effective when sober. She encourages couples to have one highly structured conversation about their life and relationship each week.

Perhaps I notice it more now I'm sober, but I don't think I've been on a night out when I haven't seen a couple have cross words, or sometimes even a shouting match in the street. But that still begs the question of why we are so up for an argument when we've been drinking.

While alcohol lowers our inhibitions and makes us a little more loose-lipped, it seems that this can come with the pitfall of being more likely to say something we don't mean or wish we hadn't. 'Sometimes, people only have the courage to mention problems after a drink, or just blurt things out and then regret it,' Cate said. And, of course, 'An awful lot of socializing is based around alcohol, so many arguments begin during or after a night out.'

But are drunken arguments an indication of deep underlying problems in a relationship? Cate said this is a hard question, because habitual drinking can creep up, and it follows that many people with serious drinking problems share drinking as an interest, and will continue to use alcohol as a way of taking care of themselves without learning how supportive the relationship itself can be.

'Though sometimes people begin drinking because their relationship is so awful,' she added, 'often the drinking disguises issues that could be addressed if having a glass of wine wasn't less trouble! Unfortunately, having a drink is also often a make-up strategy, so this can lead to more conflict, giving the impression that the relationship is in trouble rather than that the drinking is unhelpful.'

From personal experience of drunkenly unleashing things I had been holding on to for a while (pretending that I was fine with something my partner had done and then explosively declaring after a few drinks that I was definitely not fine, for instance), I do think that drunken fights can signify deeper problems. On the flip side, I also know that sometimes this is definitely not the case, making this topic a little tricky to unpick.

As part of my research for this book, I asked my followers for some of the most ridiculous reasons they'd ended up in a drunken row with their significant other. Here are some of their anecdotes.

'I refused to take off a jumper before going to bed, even though I always get too hot.'

'Because I was eating a plain tortilla in bed.'

'We were arguing about the electric toothbrush I got them for Christmas.'

> *'Because they didn't cross the street at the same time as me.'*

> *'I demanded a taxi home when we lived around the corner.'*

And my absolute number-one favourite:

> *'They had rollerblades in their bag from earlier in the day and it made me angry for no reason.'*

An interesting study conducted by the University of Bristol concluded that heightened aggression while intoxicated is not simply the result of the disinhibiting effects of alcohol. It showed that drunk people can misinterpret emotional expressions. Researchers showed pictures of different facial expressions to participants and found that they misread some non-threatening expressions (such as disgust) as threatening ones (such as anger). Interestingly, the findings were strongest in males.[1]

Could it be that your feigned disgust at your partner's cheesy dance moves was misinterpreted? Did they take it as you goading them into an argument? Quite possibly. It could also explain why I once shouted at an ex-boyfriend because he was staring at other people in a club. His defence the morning after was that he was so drunk he couldn't see straight. It's possible that what I perceived as a pervy leer was actually him struggling to keep his eyelids open.

Drunken arguments might range from silly to severe, but Cate Campbell was very clear that they can have a longer-lasting impact on the relationship. They mask problems beyond the night on which they occur and prevent couples from dealing with the underlying issues. She also said that during drunken rows there's a greater risk of violence, accidents and things being said (such as hurtful insults), which are all difficult to recover from.

This all makes a pretty compelling case that simply taking alcohol out of the equation can do wonders for your relationship. Cate agreed: 'Not drinking is a relatively easy thing for couples to do to instantly improve their communication and reduce arguments.'

Establishing boundaries

Much like in your friendships or when you're dating, setting boundaries around alcohol in romantic relationships is key to honouring your sobriety. Amanda White is a licensed therapist and owner of the Therapy for Women Center in Philadelphia, and has built a strong community on Instagram, where she shares tools for growth and healing. She's also teetotal and was therefore the perfect person to talk to about why it's so important for people on their sober journey to set such boundaries.

Amanda said, '[It's] incredibly important because it allows us to clearly communicate what we want and need.' She also noted that setting boundaries early on is paramount for success.

I know from conversations I've had with girls at SGS events that a lot of them find it triggering when their partner drinks, so I was intrigued to know how you can set boundaries around alcohol without looking like you're forcing someone to change their behaviour. Amanda explained, 'Boundaries are an internal choice we make for ourselves about something we need. This is very different than a punishment or trying to make someone change.

However, sometimes they can look the same on the outside. So checking your intentions is important.'

As expected, communication is crucial and Amanda emphasized that it's very important that your significant other understands that these boundaries are coming from something you need. 'Make sure to share with your significant other why this is important for you,' she said, 'and why this will help you as a person, and potentially even the relationship. This is an important first step before even setting the boundaries.'

Telling your loved one that you're uncomfortable with something they're doing is easier said than done. Plus, there's always the fear that they might not be receptive to change. I gave Amanda the example of not wanting to have alcohol kept in the house when the other person does. In the case of this particular conflict, she said some boundary negotiation might need to happen: 'This might mean that alcohol is kept somewhere separate in the house, your significant other doesn't drink around you in the house and goes into a separate room, or they don't keep alcohol at home for the first few months of your sobriety.'

Amanda recognized that setting these kind of boundaries is difficult, especially if two people share a home, but she explained that this is when it's important for the sober person to inspire and support their significant other, and understand that it will ultimately benefit them in the long term.

Without boundaries, resentment is absolutely going to happen. It's important that people learn how to communicate and express how they feel and get curious about why they might be feeling this way. With boundaries, often this feeling is reduced, but there may still be jealousy and annoyance. It can be helpful to remember that boundaries can be modified and changed as the relationship changes. You may need more support or firmer boundaries or less depending on what's going on in your life.

Moral of the story: if you don't have any boundaries, get some.

Wanting extra support

Perhaps you're a drinker and you're reading this book to support a partner through their sobriety. If that's the case, I applaud you.

If, on the other hand, you're struggling to make it clear to your significant other how you need to be supported in sobriety, then much like the list for your friends, here are some thoughts you can pop in front of your partner.

♥ Tell me that you're proud of me.

♥ Remember and celebrate the milestones with me. In a way, they're a bigger deal than my birthday!

♥ Take the time to understand why I'm doing this and don't dismiss it as a temporary thing.

♥ Try new alcohol-free drinks with me.

♥ If you're fixing yourself an alcoholic drink, please make me a non-alcoholic one too – I still need to stay hydrated!

♥ Please don't roll your eyes or say things like, 'That mocktail was nearly the same price as my cocktail!' And don't berate me for buying Diet Coke in a glass bottle rather than from the tap. It still doesn't cost as much as your booze, and it's worth its weight in gold to me.

- Let's go out for a monthly mocktail night. I can still go for a fancy meal or drinks, even if they're non-alcoholic.

- If you're doing the food shopping, buy nice soft drinks for me that you think I might like.

- Tell me that you think I'm still as fun/sexy/cool when sober!

- If you're seeing positive changes in me, tell me! They're great motivation boosters.

- Give me a hug when I say that I'm struggling. Some days will be harder for me than others.

- Offer to do the occasional night out with our friends without drinking so that I'm not the odd one out.

- Don't expect me to drive all the time. Just because I can, doesn't mean I want a new career as your personal Uber.

A change of heart

I've had a fair few lightbulb moments in sobriety, when it suddenly dawns on me that something no longer gives me joy now that I'm sober. The opposite also happens, when something I used to hate when I was drinking suddenly becomes enjoyable. Here are a few examples:

- Things that no longer bring me joy: house music, McDonald's and false eyelashes.

♥ Things that now bring me joy: science documentaries, coffee shops and watching people hug at airports.

For some people, a lightbulb moment can mean a realization about a specific person, or even a whole group of people. For SGS girl Bailye, her lightbulb moment was uncovering her true sexual preference: 'Before sobriety I loved men, but now my sexual preference is unique. I am so attracted to men and women – humans!' She believes that without alcohol, your true self tells you what you want.

But it's not all positive. Sometimes, sobriety can signal the end of some relationships. For Victoria, it brought with it the recognition that alcohol was the main thing that she and her ex-boyfriend had in common. Interestingly, this normally happens when only one person gets sober, but both Victoria and her boyfriend gave up drinking at the same time.

'In the beginning it was really good, but as time went on I became happier and more productive, but unfortunately he went in the other direction. He didn't want to do anything and there were a lot of arguments,' Victoria says. It was difficult to call time, but with twelve months of sobriety under her belt she had the courage to realize what was important to her: 'I'm simply not settling for someone who doesn't treat me the way I deserve or need.'

Infidelity

In 2019, a survey by iD Mobile showed how Brits were more loyal to their phone network than to their significant other, by revealing that one in ten of us is cheating on our current partner. Perhaps not a revolutionary discovery, but here's the interesting bit. The survey went on to outline the top ten reasons why people are unfaithful. Top of the list was boredom, second was feeling unloved/neglected, and in third place – shocking, but somehow not surprising – was because they were drunk at the time.

More people cheated on their significant other because they were intoxicated than because they felt they had grown apart, or because they were no longer attracted to them, or even because they'd fallen in love with someone else.

I say it wasn't a surprising finding because, over the years, countless numbers of my friends have been on the receiving end of a drunk cheater, and when I asked my followers if they thought drinking makes someone more likely to cheat, 391 out of the 425 who responded said yes.

While a lot of people I've spoken to about this believe alcohol isn't an excuse to cheat on someone, some of them expressed that they felt it's easier to forgive someone for cheating if you know they were drunk when it happened. The thing is, I know that not all drunk people cheat, but I also know that not all drunk cheating comes from a place of unhappiness – alcohol leads to reduced inhibitions and really can make us do things we'd never dream of doing sober.

The evidence is there: alcohol is shown to affect the pre-frontal cortex, which is responsible for our decision-making. This is the part of the brain that weighs up the risks and benefits of doing something harmful, and in the presence of alcohol it's essentially compromised. You can't make optimal decisions, and it's much harder to tell the difference between right and wrong.

However, it's important to clarify that while alcohol might make you do something out of character, drinking enough to get to that point is a choice that you make, so you should always take responsibility for your actions.

One thing sobriety has allowed me to do is hold up a particularly key end of the bargain in relationships – being faithful. (Disclaimer, not all relationships need to be monogamous – that's just how I do it – but the important part is that you respect whatever agreement you have in place with the other person/people you're involved with.)

Sobriety (generally) means no blurred lines, no regretful mistakes, no fuzzy memories or anxious worries that you crossed inappropriate boundaries or overstepped the mark. You're more likely to be in a place to hold yourself accountable, stay true to your values, and act in a way that aligns with your morals and beliefs. You have a clarity when it comes to your judgement, which can prevent situations that may cause feelings of guilt or shame – both of which can lead us to drink more.

Sobriety, for me, is being in control – not in a regimented, 'never let my hair down' way, but more like an 'in charge of my own destiny and how I treat the people I care about, as well as being responsible for my actions' way. I like my pre-frontal cortex firmly uncompromised.

Heartbreak

Pretty much since the dawn of time, the narrative we have been sold as young women – and men, but especially women – is that when you get your heart broken, when you feel at your lowest or your most insecure, you must immediately get dressed up, go out and get absolutely, horrendously shit-faced until you can no longer feel pain. From experience I can report this numbness lasts for approximately 4 hours, until you find yourself sobbing in a kebab shop, demanding that your friends explain why they think you got dumped as you snivel your way through a polystyrene box of undercooked cheesy chips.

A few years back, gifting brand Firebox released a gin liqueur called F*ckboy Tears, with the tagline 'empowerment is best served on the rocks'. The description on the website declares, 'All that sweet retribution turned their salty tears into a juicy passion-fruit and mango-flavoured glittery gin liqueur ... Swirl their tears around your glass to unlock a torrential wash of holographic shimmer, knowing no fuckboy is gonna mess you around again.' There was also a warning. Not a warning to 'drink responsibly' but one explaining that drinking too much of it 'may lead to rogue ex-texting'.

This normalization of drinking culture and the perpetuation of a narrative that the answer to heartache is drowning yourself in alcohol is both problematic and dangerous. It's something that I think needs to change pretty swiftly, and I think we need to hold more brands like Firebox accountable for quite obviously profiting from the vulnerability of young women. Really, sobriety is kind of like sticking two fingers up to every company that tries to insinuate that alcohol will fix our problems and make us feel better so that they can make a quick buck.

Obviously this is a subject close to my heart, so I reached out to the host of the podcast *How to Get Over Your Ex*, break-up coach Dorothy Johnson, to find out why so many of us turn to booze to get over a broken heart – aside from the fact that alcohol companies have made us believe that we need to.

Dorothy confirmed what I already know, which is that a lot of people turn to booze as a coping mechanism during a break-up.

Typically, after a break-up we feel sad, depressed, angry, betrayed, and sometimes even resentful. These emotions are caused by our thoughts and perceptions, and after a break-up we are *constantly* thinking about our ex, our past with them, and the visions of our imagined future with them. Our thoughts and feelings are being consumed by our ex. And most people don't know that 1) thoughts create our feelings, not our ex and what they did or didn't do; and 2) we are in control of what we think, and thoughts are optional.

So that they can remain fully in control of their thoughts and feelings, Dorothy advises clients to eliminate alcohol from their lives – or at least decrease their consumption – during her three-month programme.

She went on to explain, 'When we feel so out of control, we think that "distractions" like alcohol can stop us from feeling so shitty,' which, she says, sadly isn't true. 'I compare it to holding a beach ball under water – eventually it will resurface. Drinking is only a partial solution to feeling a negative emotion. True relief is addressing the root cause, the key to which lies in managing your mind, the thoughts you have about your break-up, and how you're viewing yourself in this narrative.'

I've always fallen for the idea that distractions such as alcohol work, and Dorothy explained that this is because we're just thinking new thoughts. When we're stuck at home, we're running over the same old things in our mind – what our ex did to us, what they didn't apologize for, and wondering whether they're doing fine without us – but then we go out with the girls and our thoughts are different. We think about new possibilities, how we like our outfits and that we might just be OK, so we generate different emotions.

Generating different emotions sounds like a good thing to me, but this is where it gets tricky. Dorothy explained, 'The only problem with choosing drink as your specific distraction from negative emotions is that it typically leads to more depressive thoughts later in the evening, unless you black out, in which case you aren't even consciously aware of your thoughts.' She's right – drinking definitely used to help me for the first couple of hours, but anything after that definitely did not.

I confessed to Dorothy how I felt bad that I'd spent a while ignoring my feelings after a break-up rather than dealing with them, and that I think this set me back in my 'grieving process'. While she agreed that drinking prolongs the 'grief', she also argued that it was still part of my process and it was still a step forward in my heartbreak journey, which got me to where I am now – sober and happy.

This made me feel a lot better about the months I wasted getting blackout drunk. Dorothy made me realize that had I not gone through any of that, then I might not have embraced sobriety, and that decision remains the best one I've ever made.

Dorothy challenges her clients to think about what would happen if, instead of channelling their energy into drinking and making their life seem better, they could put that energy towards actually making their reality better. This is pretty much the question I asked myself the morning I decided to give up drinking. Looking back now, I wish I'd had someone like Dorothy who could have headed my six-month meltdown off at the pass, but here are some tips you could use to prevent yours:

- Feel your negative emotions, lean inwards and ask yourself how your emotions actually make you feel. Ask yourself how they look, what colour are they?

- Acknowledge that this break-up happened for you, not to you (this is Dorothy's go-to break-up motto)

- Experience new things

- Realize that nothing has gone wrong

- Hire a coach/therapist, if you are able to

- Ask yourself what you can learn from staying open to this experience with grace

- Treat the coming weeks and months as time to transform who you are, because it can change the trajectory of your life

- Meditate

- Travel, if you can

- Know deep down in your bones that your life can, and will, be better than the one you had with your ex

Dorothy's words are exactly what I needed to hear over three years ago, when I was slamming tequilas trying to mend my broken heart. Even now that I'm pretty far into sobriety, the prospect of having to deal with a break-up in the future still terrifies me. I asked Dorothy for her advice on how to ensure you don't fall back into a habit of drinking, should you find yourself in such a situation again.

The biggest thing, she said, is to recognize that by drinking, all you would be doing is avoiding experiencing a negative emotion. She encourages anyone to ask themselves, 'What would it be like to experience a negative emotion and not let it dictate my entire day? What would it be like to use that negative emotion to fuel the creation of a life that I'd never thought possible?' She offered the following words of encouragement:

> Identify that emotion, understand what thoughts are creating that emotion, and then redirect to thoughts that create a different emotional experience for you. Instead of numbing and distracting yourself, what would it be like to be *alive* for your whole life? The good, the bad, the better, and the amazing?

Everything Dorothy said throughout our interview made me feel empowered to take on the world, but this final piece of advice particularly stuck with me: 'A break-up can shape you, either in a good way or a bad way, and you always have the power and the control. So, in what way do you want a break-up to shape you? Do the work on *you*. Change *you* so that you don't keep recreating old patterns and treat the root cause of all of these things – the heartbreak and the drinking.'

Sober Girl Gains

- [ ] Less chance of impulsive infidelity
- [ ] Falling in love with yourself
- [ ] Fun dates that involve something other than drinks
- [ ] Healing your heartbreak without distraction
- [ ] A new and fully functioning dickhead detector – you can't get those on eBay!

8

Let's Talk About (Sober) Sex, Baby

The booze-free birds and the bees

As someone who was knee-tremblingly terrified about how she would even kiss someone on a date without a little Dutch courage, I can tell you that the idea of sober sex seemed completely unfathomable to me when I first stopped drinking. I'd go as far as to say that it's probably one of the reasons why I didn't stop sooner. And I actually think a lot of people feel the same, and not just if they're single.

In 2013, a survey showed that one in ten couples in the UK admitted that they hadn't had sex without being under the influence of alcohol in over six months, and more than half of them claimed that they simply 'aren't in the mood' unless under the influence either.[1] So, could it be that alcohol makes us more 'up for it'?

I checked back in with Cate Campbell, who said, 'Alcohol use is associated with celebration and relaxation, which may be very significant. The feeling of being "off duty" signified by alcohol use, and the context (a date or a birthday, for example), may be the reason for choosing to have sex rather than being blotto.' This isn't something I'd really thought of, but perhaps for a lot of us, especially those in long-term relationships, these sorts of celebrations (usually tied to alcohol) come with a sense of obligation to spend a passionate night between the sheets.

Psychologist Simon Parritt identifies association as a possible reason for this.[2] He believes that our first experiences of alcohol tend to coincide with our early sexual experiences rather than occasions of celebration, and so it's likely that the brain has forged an association between alcohol and sex from an early age. He also thinks that, for women in particular, 'having a heart-to-heart is a huge aphrodisiac and that may be more likely when you've both had a couple of drinks'. While I hate to think it's true, getting into deep conversations with someone and connecting with them on an emotional level is probably one of the quickest ways to get me into bed.

Now, all these explanations seem pretty solid to me, but I'd like to throw in what I believe was the biggest reason I needed to drink before dropping my knickers: alcohol helped me to feel less insecure.

From stressing that I'd put on weight and worrying that I wasn't sexy enough, to feeling vulnerable wearing new lingerie in case I didn't get the reaction I wanted – booze always seemed like the best way to give me an instant confidence boost in the bedroom, and I began to feel like I needed it to take my clothes off in front of another person.

Cate Campbell explained that when people need to be drunk to have sex, the problem isn't alcohol – it's the relationship, a lack of experience, unhelpful beliefs or trauma associated with sex. I guess some of my initial insecurities fell into several of these categories – my unhelpful belief that I needed to look like Jennifer Lopez to have great sex being one, and my lack of experience in sleeping with people sober being another. So that gives us a rough idea of why a lot of us need alcohol to really get randy. But could booze be creating bigger issues in the bedroom?

The problem with people drinking before doing the deed is that when people are drunk, they aren't as aware of what's happening to them or what they're doing, and they're not as receptive to mood and sensation, Cate went on to say.

Interestingly, almost half of the participants in the 2013 survey confessed that intoxicated intercourse had negatively affected their sex lives. A whopping three-quarters of participants admitted that the quality of sex they were having while under the influence was 'poor' and two-fifths claimed that alcohol had caused their 'sexual performance' to suffer.

While drunk sex is another part of the alcohol effect that's consistently glamorized on the big and small screens, it seems that the reality of a boozy bonk is often quite different to what they show in films and on TV. How many times have you left a bar to go home and immediately done it in the doorway of the other person's house? Where's the awkward taxi ride, the chat about protection, the moment you realize that alcohol doesn't always enhance performance, or the bit when you both pass out before you even get started?

Cate said that a common issue for men is to experience an episode of erectile difficulty – often attributable to alcohol use – and then be so afraid of it happening again that the person drinks more to overcome their anxiety about it, so it happens again and a pattern develops. I can't help but reflect on situations where I've been on the *pardon me* receiving end of this and, being drunk and irrational, my self-esteem definitely took a swift nosedive. It's not really an ideal situation for anyone to be in.

According to Cate, the same sort of thing happens when sex is painful, especially for women. 'When you're drinking,' she told me, 'it's harder to become aroused and orgasm, making sex less pleasant. So someone might think they need a drink to make it better when they actually need not to.'

This all sounds like a vicious cycle we're best off out of, but getting comfortable with the notion of sober sex doesn't just happen overnight – it takes a while and it takes boosting your confidence in areas outside of the bedroom too. If you're already stressing about getting your kit off for the first time in front of a new (or even current) love interest, or you need a helping hand to get horny, here are some cheeky pointers to get you started.

Love Yourself

Sobriety is the perfect time to rediscover what you like in all areas of your life, and that includes your sex life too. If sober sex isn't happening for you, or maybe you're not ready to take the plunge, then why not get to know what really gets you going first?

Almost as underrated a self-care method as sobriety, not only is masturbation free but it also boasts a whole host of benefits that might give your sobriety a mischievous boost.

Despite the myths, there are no physical harmful side effects of masturbation. It's a healthy, fun and normal act. However, before you add that bullet to your basket, I need to add the disclaimer that masturbating excessively can harm your relationships and everyday life, so that's something to keep in mind. While I'm not suggesting that masturbation alone will keep you sober, it does offer some of the same benefits that alcohol promises, but without the hangover and the morning-after regret.

Increases confidence

If you've become used to having numbed-out, drunk sex, then it's possible you have no idea what you really like or haven't had the opportunity to acknowledge that this might have changed. Knowing how to pleasure yourself can increase your confidence, which you can take into the bedroom with you when you feel the time is right.

Relieves stress and boosts mood

Two pretty big drinking triggers are stress and sadness, so masturbation can be *ahem* handy for both. Not only does the act of masturbation cause the pleasure chemical dopamine to be released, but hitting the big O releases the hormone oxytocin, which in turn lowers cortisol (the stress hormone) levels.

Pain relief

Whether it's menstrual cramps or a bad back, a lot of people turn to alcohol for a quick pain fix – so might a little self-love work instead? A study from the University of Münster in Germany showed that approximately 60 per cent of respondents who engaged in sexual activity during a migraine reported relief, which leads to the assumption that orgasm can be a key factor in pain relief as a result of the endorphins released during climax.[3]

Better sleep

Having trouble nodding off without your usual nightcap? That climax chemical oxytocin creates an overall feeling of relaxation. Vasopressin, another chemical associated with sleep, is also released during orgasm.

Enhances your libido

Two separate studies found that vibrator use has been linked to an increase in desire, arousal and overall sexual function, and women also reported an increase in lubrication levels.[4] If you're encountering a lack of libido without alcohol in your life, showing yourself a good time first might be worth a go.

A self-pleasure newbie? Check out the support and resources at the end of the book (see page 281).

Sober Girl Spotlight
'I stopped drinking and reclaimed my sexual power.'

Africa Brooke (@africabrooke) stopped drinking in 2016 at the age of twenty-four, after it became glaringly obvious that it was starting to cause chaos for both herself and those around her: 'I was losing friends. I had a fractured relationship with my family, and my partner at the time gave me an ultimatum because my blackouts were fuelling too many arguments and were creating distrust in our relationship.'

Even though she had made seven attempts to get sober in the past, Africa tried once more because she knew that if she didn't, 'I would lose everyone and everything I had, including my life.'

Like for so many of us, alcohol was present the first time Africa had sex at the age of fourteen, and she believes this established a belief that she needed to be drunk or have alcohol in her system to have sex confidently. 'From that time up until when I got sober, I was no stranger to unprotected casual sex. I would wake up in strange beds not knowing whether I'd had sex or not, and would cheat on partners. It was an absolute disaster!'

Africa says that she used to feel immense shame after pleasuring her own body. It was as if she had done something 'bad' or 'wrong', but a year into her sobriety she started to learn about taking a tantric (slower and intentional) approach to sex: 'I was finally able to get to know my body in ways that I thought only sexual partners could. Self-pleasure is what led me on the journey to sexual liberation, and I highly doubt I would be on this path if I hadn't released alcohol from my life.'

In 2017, Africa started the Cherry Revolution (@cherryrevolution), a sexual wellness company whose house mantra is 'DEATH TO FAKING IT'. She set it up as a healing tool for her own sexual awakening and for that of women and vulva owners all over the world: 'I realized that even though many of us have been having sex for a long time, we feel shame when talking about it. We feel like we don't have autonomy over our bodies and our pleasure. My life-long mission is to show women that it is safe to explore the fullness of who we are. And sex is no exception!'

Africa says that to describe her relationship with sex in sobriety as the complete opposite to what it was would be an understatement.

I now have the most beautiful relationship with my sexuality and my body. Without the haze of alcohol and drugs I've been able to get to the bottom of the sexual shame I was holding. I experiment safely and mindfully with trusted partners, I own all parts of myself – even those I'm still learning to love fully – and I give myself full permission to have conversations about sex from a place of curiosity and a willingness to learn.

Africa thinks that it can take some time to feel desire and pleasure in sobriety, especially if you've been used to numbing yourself. She's quick to assert that feeling doesn't last for ever, and you don't have to push your body to do things it isn't ready for yet.

You are likely to feel a lot of emotions as you meet the most vulnerable parts of yourself, which is why self-compassion and kindness are key. As you get to meet a new version of yourself in clarity, you will also get the chance to get clear about your needs, your desires, your noes – and you will unearth the voice that will help you in making those things known so you can set necessary boundaries and explore your sexuality, safely.

Boost Your Confidence Outside the Bedroom

When I gave up drinking I went back to dancing, I faced my fears on a zip-wire, I started going to work without wearing make-up, I went on holiday on my own and, in time, even sober dating gave me a confidence boost (once I realized it wasn't like setting myself on fire). Little by little you'll realize that real and authentic confidence is built by making it through scary situations without booze. Every time you feel the fear and do it anyway, you can say, 'I know I survived it without booze before, so next time perhaps it won't be as bad.'

Get Sex Education

The positives of sober sex are hard to ignore, and while some are weighted more towards the emotional side of things, there's plenty of science to back up the benefits of a sober session.

Wet, wet, wet

Even if your drinking habits aren't dry, you might be. Sexual arousal needs a certain volume of blood to bring oxygen and greater sensation to the genitals – it's how we self-lubricate. Unfortunately, thanks to booze, there won't be as much liquid in the body and your nervous system will be depressed, so you may struggle. As Cate noted earlier, intercourse can become quite painful.

Bigger and more frequent orgasms

Orgasms quite literally happen in the brain, so drinking can dampen the sexual response and decrease the intensity of your orgasm. It's also harder to climax, so you can probably kiss any chance of a multiple goodbye.

Frisky but less risky

Many studies have shown that you are more likely to have unprotected sex if you've been drinking, and there's a huge link between STDs and alcohol consumption. Having a sexually transmitted infection is definitely nothing to be ashamed of, but some can be extremely serious and others, if left untreated, can have long-term health implications. Safe sex is best!

No bumps in the night

Drinking impairs your reaction times – it's the main reason there are so many rules about getting behind the wheel – and it's worth noting that accidents and misjudgements aren't exclusive to driving. Over the years, some pretty shocking drunken sex injuries have been reported to the medical community. One doctor claims that penile fractures usually happen when a partner is drunk and, er . . . passionately over-thrusts.

Connection

If you're not one for cringey sentiments, brace yourself. When you use alcohol to numb yourself, you cannot select which emotions to dampen. When you use alcohol as a defensive shield against the rawer emotions you might experience during sex, such as insecurity or awkwardness, you risk numbing out all the good bits too. You can miss tender moments, the beauty of being vulnerable, or the exchanges of deep unclouded connection. Without alcohol your emotions will be heightened, but there is such a beauty in that. From personal experience, the sex I have now is on a deeper level, and I feel in tune with my emotions, body and my partner at all times.

Be Honest and Communicate

When it comes to sexual encounters, you can't really dictate how much the other person drinks beforehand, but personally I find the whole experience much more satisfying when your partner is sober too. After my own experiences of sex where the issue of consent wasn't exactly crystal clear, I have a heightened awareness that I might be taking advantage of my partner if they've been drinking. The key is to be honest early on and feel free to disclose how important clear communication is to you and the reasons why.

When I was younger I remember hearing that if you're not mature enough to overcome your embarrassment and buy condoms, then you shouldn't be having sex. I kind of think the same is true here. If you don't feel comfortable enough with someone to air your concerns or preferences early on, perhaps you shouldn't be having sex with them.

There's also nothing wrong with admitting that you're nervous. You don't have to take off your clothes with all the charisma of a burlesque dancer, and admitting your vulnerability can be a pretty magical thing. Cate Campbell agrees, saying, 'Be emphatic about wanting to enjoy every second instead of being drowsy or distracted by alcohol. Talk about this first, rather than cross your fingers and hope it will be OK.'

Listen to the People Who Have Been There

When I asked SGS girls how sex had changed for them since ditching the drink, the responses flowed along the same lines. For those who are settled and have had to embrace their existing relationship with a clearer head, the general consensus was that sex initially felt more intimidating but it was worth it.

> *'I feel less confident, but the connection between me and my fiancé is so much stronger.'*
>
> *'Initiating sex is harder but the sex is so so so much better.'*
>
> *'I feel more present during sex. I'm able to hold a deeper connection throughout and afterwards.'*
>
> *'I've learned that I am allowed to enjoy it and my pleasure is just as important as my partner's.'*

For those who are single and sober, it's clear that the benefits aren't as instant, but many women remarked that, over time, sex without booze came into its own.

> *'At first: scary, embarrassing. Now: more pleasurable and never regretted.'*
>
> *'It has meaning. When I was drinking, I was so detached from my own body and so also from sex.'*
>
> *'I'm more honest about my wants, and respect my boundaries and body more.'*

'There are no more blurred regretful encounters, it is now beautiful, fantastic and intimate.'

And by far my favourite response about how powerfully sobriety can affect your sex life:

'I am finally working and healing through my issues with sexual intimacy, and learning how to feel safe.'

Realize It Might Be Quality Over Quantity

Just between us girlfriends, one-night stands dwindled for me in early sobriety. It's not to say they were non-existent but essentially, the less I got the booze out, the less I got my boobs out. While I'm still a champion for anyone who's got the guts to roll in the hay with someone they've just met, I found that without a bit of boozed-up bravado it took me at least three or four dates until I was comfortable with the thought of that person seeing me naked.

This opens up lots of questions about consent, which I'm still trying to untangle. If I needed a few drinks to have sex with someone, was it really consensual? Is drunk sex ever consensual?

I put this question to Kristina Sperkova, who is a psychologist, alcohol policy advocate, development aid specialist, feminist, civil society activist, human rights defender and humanist. She is also the first female international president of Movendi International, which is the largest global movement tackling all aspects of alcohol harm. Kristina said it's actually a very philosophical issue, but she believes there should be one main question asked: Would I have sex with this person, right here and right now, if alcohol wasn't involved? If the answer is yes, it can be considered consensual. If the answer is no, or doubtful, it is not consensual.

I don't think there are any exceptions to this reasoning, even if it relates to a long-term partner, even if yesterday you would have said yes but today you wouldn't. If it wouldn't be a hell yes, then it's a hell no.

Sober Girl Gains

☐ Breaking the association between booze and bonking

☐ Getting to know yourself – intimately!

☐ Bigger and better big orgasms

☐ Less chance of a mortifying sexual mishap!

☐ A deeper sexual connection to yourself and other people

9

Soberly Ever After

The hurdles, pitfalls and magical milestones

I f I could pass on everything I have learned about sobriety, I'd need more than the space allocated for this book, and believe me when I say that I really learn something new every day. Still, I hope to cover in this chapter the rest of the major hurdles that you will encounter should you choose to quit or cut down on your drinking. What follows should answer the rest of your burning questions, but if it doesn't, check out the support and resources section (see pages 279–289) where I've included lots more information for you to follow up at your leisure.

Change Your Mindset

It's paramount to try to see sobriety as a gain and not a loss. Rather than looking at it as deprivation, it's important to recognize that it's actually about wealth and abundance. I choose to see sobriety as removing an obstacle that's stopping me from getting to all the good stuff, such as amazing sleep and shame-free Sundays.

I am constantly trying to find the positives of sobriety in any situation, whether that's 'Thank heavens I'm not going to embarrass myself at this very important work drinks' or 'I'm so glad I don't need to spend money on cocktails tonight and can instead buy that overpriced eye palette, of which I'll certainly only use one shade.' Sobriety is an advantage, not a disadvantage, and for everything that you think you're giving up in alcohol, you really are gaining something else in sobriety, be that time, money, not having to wee every five minutes, or never ever having a hangover. Your mindset is everything, so this is the best place to begin.

Shake Up Your Habits

In the early days of sobriety, I lived by three mottos I think really helped me to fall in love with my new lifestyle. They were:

Do stuff that scares you

Every time I've broken up with a boyfriend, I've treated myself to a new piercing. I couldn't say for sure what compels me to do it, but I think it's a mixture of rebellion, marking a new era of change, and proving to myself that I don't need someone to hold my hand through the scary things – that I'm quite able to suck it up, push myself out of my comfort zone and face the pain alone.

During early sobriety I adopted a similar mindset and did lots of scary things – I went on sober dates, I started going to new classes, I did a zip-wire, and I met up with sober strangers off the internet to prove to myself that I can do nerve-racking things without someone (or in this case something) always having my back. Those things proved to me that I didn't always need alcohol to step out of my comfort zone.

I'm not encouraging anyone to put holes in their body or do anything they really don't want to. However, if there's something you've toyed with doing but are too scared to make the leap without alcohol – leap anyway. I constantly hear people say things like, 'I'd love to cut down/quit drinking, but I couldn't possibly do XYZ sober!' But what if you tried? What if you did it and you had a great time? What if you did it once just to see?

The bottom line is when you use alcohol to get through scary or uncomfortable situations (dating, dancing, and so on), you don't build any real confidence. In fact, I'd argue it makes you less confident because you begin to rely on alcohol to do those things. *But*, every time you make it through a scary situation sober, you build so much genuine belief in yourself. You put a little tick on your scary checklist and you start to think that yes, you probably can do it and you just keep doing it. Then, before you know it, those things that seemed really scary don't seem that bad any more.

Do more random stuff

For a lot of us drinking is a habit, something we do without question and without really examining our motivations. It's just a part of life – no different to brushing your teeth or your morning injection of caffeine. I've found that the thing that makes breaking a habit the hardest is when it fits so seamlessly into my routine. For me, the best way to break a habit is to mix up my life by doing completely random and out-of-the-ordinary things. What did I do on the first weekend of sobriety? An alpaca trek and feed in the middle of the Kentish countryside.

What I've also found is that the more novel and random the activity, the better. The further from your routine the activity is, the less you'll associate it with drinking. Have you been to aerial yoga before? No? Great, that means you won't have drunk wine there before, you won't associate wine with that activity, and it won't become a habit to have wine if you choose to do that activity again.

In early sobriety, I also went white-water rafting in the UK, bear-watching from a boat in Canada, and axe-throwing – none of which involved alcohol. I'd say this is definitely a wise decision when you're chucking sharp instruments at a target.

Do more stuff on your own

Before my granny passed away, she often went to the cinema on her own. I always found it a bit weird, mainly because I always cared too much about what people thought about me, and God forbid anyone ever saw me enjoying popcorn and a rom-com in public on my lonesome. But here's the thing about not drinking: you will never make it work unless you stop caring what people think.

Although the majority of people in my life have come around to the idea of my sobriety and are so very supportive, I'd be lying if I said that I didn't still come across the odd person who says that I'm boring or makes some basic joke about not being able to trust people who don't drink. (By the way, this doesn't make sense to me. We'll never drive you drunk and we won't spill all your secrets after a tequila!)

When I started to realize that someone would always have something to say about my not drinking, I realized that meant that they would always have something to say about me too. I decided that my granny had been on to something in never caring what people thought when she was spotted doing stuff on her own.

The second strand to this is that when I gave up drinking I was single, and so I suddenly found myself with a lot of time and a lot of things I wanted to do. Understandably, I was pretty disgruntled when all my friends and family didn't *immediately* drop their plans to accommodate me and my new-found excitement for life.

Eventually, I stopped waiting around and just started doing the things I wanted to do – alone. I've been to the cinema on my own, to dinner on my own, and to classes on my own. I've travelled solo and then I started running brunches and events for girls like me who didn't want to wait around any more. My advice is to book the tickets, book the class and book the flights. Do the things you never had time for – even if no one else will do them with you.

Surviving the Everyday

Big milestone events can feel complex and daunting. It's therefore absolutely imperative to prepare for them, but sometimes a craving for a drink can smack you in the face when you least expect it.

Ironically, you might be absolutely fine at your mate's wedding, surrounded by free-flowing fizz, but one Tuesday night, when you're minding your own business and catching up on *RuPaul's Drag Race*, a hankering for a glass of chilled pinot grigio may wash over you like a boozy wave.

For that reason, it's always good to be prepared. While it might sound exhausting, you can simply put a few key changes in place for when this moment inevitably strikes.

Don't have drink in the house

This one's relatively easy – the more obstacles you can put between yourself and easy access to a drink, the better. Sometimes the physical distance alone can give you enough time for the craving to pass.

Change up your everyday routine

Perhaps Thirsty Thursdays are your thing, perhaps you have a Saturday-lunch ritual of wine with the girls. Either way, switching up your routine, especially for the first few weeks (or months), can really help. Commitment is a good one here: book a class or schedule in something you won't want to cancel. If you commit to it financially, you're also more likely to stick to it.

Do something first

If you get a craving, do anything else imaginable first: have a bath, drink a tea, brush your teeth. Just one activity can give you a bit of thinking space to analyse your trigger rather than acting on impulse. More often than not, the craving will subside and you'll be glad that you didn't make a rash decision.

HALT, BITCH

For those who aren't already familiar with the HALT technique, this is the idea that before you reach for that wine, cigarette or ex's phone number, you ask yourself the question, 'Do I really want this or is it because I am Hungry, Angry, Lonely or Tired?' The thinking behind it is that there might be a few basic needs you actually need to address first, so maybe what you're feeling is not really about the craving at all.

I like the HALT technique, but I also think it doesn't cover everything when it comes to booze – so I've added some extra letters . . .

♥ **Bored** – do I fancy a drink because I'm bored shitless?

♥ **Isolated** – do I fancy a drink because I've had no social connection? (Clarification: this is different to feeling lonely. I believe you can feel lonely in a room full of people but isolation is when you haven't seen people physically for a while.)

♥ **Tested** – do I fancy a drink because people are calling me boring or saying I'm no fun?

♥ **Comfortable** – do I fancy a drink because I think I've cracked this whole sober thing and having one or two would be easy?

♥ **Hormonal** – do I fancy a drink or am I just a raging monster who is due on her period?

So, next time that devil on your shoulder says they fancy a drink, tell them to HALT, BITCH, and work out what's really behind the craving.

Replacement Habits

You may find, as a lot of people do, that getting rid of such a big habit from your life might lead you to replace the ritual of drinking with something else. Some people report becoming obsessed with going to the gym at the start of their sober journey, but unfortunately I wasn't that lucky.

My advice to people in early sobriety is not to stress too much. It's hard enough giving up alcohol without trying to attempt a sugar and shopping detox too. Try concentrating on giving up the booze first, and everything else will fall in place over time, once you've strengthened your sober muscles.

The Time of the Month

Ladies, researchers suspect that people who experience symptoms of premenstrual syndrome may tend to drink more alcohol just before their period – so it's worth bearing this in mind if you find that your cravings are stronger when Mother Nature comes calling.

For those who deem themselves as more sober curious than sober sober, there is some evidence to suggest that alcohol consumed during your luteal phase (the second half of your menstrual cycle) may have more of an effect on your mood than in the follicular phase.[1] It can increase feelings of both depression and anxiety while increasing feelings of enjoyment from the effects of alcohol at the same time. If you don't want alcohol to exacerbate your already temperamental mood, this might be a good time to engage in more sober behaviour.

Navigating Awkward Conversations

Being asked over and over again why you don't drink is enough to wear anyone down, so in this situation you have two options: engage or don't engage.

Usually, I find that my decision to engage is dictated by my mood or how the question is put to me. I feel like I'm pretty good at reading people, so if someone asks me inquisitively and with genuine interest why I don't drink, I'll give them the whole story. More often than not they tell me that they'd love to cut back on booze themselves. But if someone asks me in a manner that feels slightly mocking, they'll receive more of a curt reply along the lines of 'Because I don't want to'.

Where possible, I try to keep an open mind when it comes to these conversations. I see quite a few posts on Instagram that say it's no one's business why you don't drink, and although I agree to an extent, if we shut down everyone who expresses an interest in our choice, then we'll never open up the conversation and show people how amazing sobriety can be.

Even people who pose the question in a way that doesn't seem all that positive have come back to me months later to commend me on what I'm doing. I very much enjoy it when someone thinks I'm a bit boring for not drinking and then I get to see them hungover the next day. They quickly turn into the boring one while I'm smiling and laughing like a bright fucking button.

If you feel a bit more mischievous, you can always flip the question around and ask them why they do drink – there's nothing like watching someone justifying why needing booze to have fun makes them less boring than you. Or even better, you could just tell them that you read this book and it changed your life – perhaps it could change theirs too.

Taking Your Time

If you start to engage with the sober community on Instagram, you will inevitably come across the hashtag #ODAAT. Initially I thought it was something to do with the popular #OOTD (outfit of the day), but I was surprised to discover this acronym in fact stands for 'one day at a time'. A popular message used in recovery circles, the ethos is to encourage people not to feel overwhelmed by the decision to give up drinking. Instead, take each day as it comes. For some, ODAAT is the motto that has kept them sober – it's even become a popular tattoo choice.

For me, this philosophy has always felt a little open-ended, and so I simply say that I'll never drink again. When I say this, non-sober people will often respond with things like, 'Do you really want to put that kind of pressure on yourself?', 'Never say never!', 'Not even one at your wedding?' and 'You might think differently in a few years.' Additionally, sober people will make comments such as, 'Don't get ahead of yourself' or 'You really should take it one day at a time', which is proof that you can't ever please everyone.

All these points are valid: I understand that if you're in early sobriety or really struggling, the 'one day at a time' ethos might really be what's best. But for where I am now, I truly believe that I'll never have an alcoholic drink again. Not one.

I'm at the same point with booze that you get to with an ex-boyfriend/girlfriend, where you stop romanticizing them and instead begin to wonder what you saw in them in the first place. I don't ever want to go back to alcohol – not even for a night, not even for my wedding.

Saying I'll never drink again doesn't make me feel pressured, it makes me feel peaceful. It makes me recognize that I've accepted my relationship with alcohol is done, I've moved on, and now I can fully concentrate on living an alcohol-free life. To me, pressure would be having regular internal debates about whether or not I will have a drink at my wedding, regardless of the fact I'm not even due to get married. Or constantly thinking that one day I might wake up in a state of panic after an unintentional blackout or always wondering how I'll cope mentally if I ever have to endure another three-day hangover.

Eliminating the worrying element and closing the door on drinking for ever has taken away the pressure for me. That doesn't mean it's easy, but I for one find it's much easier than the constant 'will I, won't I?' conversations taking place in my head. I will never drink again and I'm totally cool with that. If you need to take it one day at a time for ever, then do what works for you.

The Drinking Dreams

Here's an interesting one: sometimes you'll go to sleep and wake up in a cold sweat because you've had a dream that you got drunk, slept with your co-worker and wrote off your car. Drinking dreams are common but a very under-researched phenomenon, so there's not really much science to go on.

From a personal perspective, I struggle to find a link between drinking dreams and my current state of mind. They happen when I'm content as much as when I'm stressed. While thankfully they're fewer and further between these days, I still experience them three years on – even people with decades of sobriety under their belt still report experiencing them. Either way, I don't believe they are an indication that my sobriety is in trouble. During the course of writing this book I've had loads, but my resolve has never felt stronger.

The best thing to do with these dreams is not to dwell on them. They don't mean you're missing booze and they don't mean you're on the verge of an imminent relapse (a term I'm not a fan of in any case). Sometimes you can get complacent in your sobriety, especially when you've forgotten what it feels like to be hungover. These days, I reframe these nightmares as great reminders, so that when I wake up in a cold sweat I'm reminded of exactly where I never want to be again.

Boozeless Beverages

From navigating no- and low-alcohol drinks menus to learning how to create delicious mocktails, here are a few things that might come in handy when navigating alcohol-free options.

0.5 per cent ABV

Some drinks are 0.5 per cent ABV or under, and you might find that some of these drinks are labelled as 'alcohol-free' or 'ultra-low alcohol'. It leaves a lot of people wondering – how can something be alcohol-free when it contains alcohol? Can I drink it if I'm sober?

Let's recap the basics first. ABV stands for 'alcohol by volume' – if a drink is 4 per cent ABV, then 4 per cent of that drink is alcohol. The rest is water and other ingredients. Now, 0.5 per cent ABV or below (trace) is basically the equivalent amount of alcohol in a pineapple, a good sourdough bread or an overripe banana. *Anything* that involves a fermentation process will contain a trace amount of alcohol – you even have that amount circulating naturally in your gut.

Will trace alcohol get you drunk? Highly unlikely. Unless you have a very rare medical condition that means you can't metabolize alcohol properly, 0.5 per cent ABV drinks will not get you drunk. You'd have to drink so much of them that you'd probably die from the vast liquid intake first.

Lots of foods, especially certain desserts like tiramisu, contain trace alcohol but don't need to be labelled because they're foods. The same goes for kombucha, a fermented tea drink. You don't need a licence to sell 0.5 per cent ABV drinks and, to add to the confusion, it depends where they're brewed as to what label they can display on them. A 0.5 per cent ABV beer from some places can be labelled alcohol-free in the UK if it is deemed so in its home country. To make matters more confusing, the rules are also grey on labelling for British brands producing overseas.

Because the non-alcoholic drinks market is fairly new, it's basically a minefield, and organizations are campaigning for consistent labelling so that it's easier to navigate. But in summary, the only reason why you shouldn't drink 0.5 per cent ABV drinks as a sober person is if you feel they are triggering. If you find that they give you a taste for the real thing, then avoid them. There are plenty of good sodas and sparkling waters available instead.

For me, they're a blessing. They are one more thing to stop me feeling left out of the celebrations, and they satisfy any craving I ever have for the real thing – they are my new normal. Unfortunately, I don't have space for all my favourite brands in this book, but I am always sharing new ones on Instagram as and when I find them.

Drinks menus

I know I don't really need to tell you how to order off a menu, but bear with me – I do have a few helpful suggestions that I hope will not come across as patronizing. First, scan the menu properly because no two are the same. Sometimes you'll find non-alcoholic beers in the soft drinks section and other times you'll find them in the beer section. The same goes for cocktails. I've complained about a lack of selection many a time only to have a very polite bartender tell me I've missed the whole section of 'softails' at the back.

My second tip is to go rogue. If you're at a cocktail bar, the mixologists should be skilled enough to whip you up something unique. It's also worth asking if there's anything that's not on the menu. One time I was at a local pub, and although I couldn't see any non-alcoholic beers on the menu, I thought I'd ask about them anyway. The bartender said I was in luck because they were actually beginning to stock them but hadn't got round to putting them on the menu yet. We then got into a ten-minute conversation about my favourite brands. They were noticing a rise in requests for non-alcoholic beers and were keen to expand their offering but genuinely had no idea where to start.

Get creative

You only need to search online for good mocktail recipes to find a host of interesting concoctions you can make from the comfort of your own kitchen. If, like me, you like a good old-fashioned recipe book, I've included my favourites in the support and resources section (see page 282).

Sober Sirens

Inevitably you'll come across people who have stricter rules for their sobriety than you do. There will be those who believe kombucha is a slippery slope to a 'relapse', and that you're destined to fail in sobriety without the twelve steps. But here's the thing: no one can police your sobriety except you. Being hard on yourself and thinking there's a right way to do things is not helpful. Ultimately, the only right way is whichever works for you.

It works in the other direction too: if you meet someone who steers clear of alcohol-free beer or doesn't want to come on your sober bar crawl, you need to respect their wishes too. In just the same way that we label ourselves, our choice on how we 'do' sobriety is our own.

Birthdays

I am a Leo, which makes me the type of person who will insist that everyone celebrates my birthday for the entire month of August. But if you're anything like some of my friends, you might not wish to acknowledge the day you entered the world at all. Either way, navigating your own birthday in sobriety can be tricky.

Really, it's entirely up to you if you'd rather gloss over the whole thing, but I normally use the opportunity to organize something fun that otherwise in the year might not have happened. One birthday was bowling, complete with Slush Puppies and karaoke.

However you decide to celebrate, make sure you acknowledge that you're entering another year with your sobriety intact, even if you're just beginning, and life has so many amazing things in store for you and your next boozeless year on the planet.

Navigating Office Parties

I've attended a few work outings sober now, and I can honestly say that they're one of the more challenging social occasions for me. These days, when I'm out with my friends, I don't ever have to justify my decision not to drink, but whenever I'm around new people or people who don't know that I'm sober, the vibe is very different. I know it's only a matter of time before someone offers me a glass of champagne and looks offended when I turn it down.

My first tip is to find other non-drinkers, the most obvious being the pregnant people or those from teetotal cultures – they are your safety net and might be finding it hard too! The second is to keep reminding yourself how relieved you'll feel the following day when you're not the subject of office gossip. While you might feel excruciatingly awkward at this party, imagine feeling ten times worse every time you bump into that 21-year-old intern in the kitchen. Yes, the one you tried to make a move on. My third bit of advice is to always French exit. Unlike disappearing on your friends during a night out, which might cause you to feel guilty and your friends to panic about your whereabouts, I can promise you that the sad reality of disappearing on a work night out is that no one will give two hoots.

The Festive Season

With the whole 'eat, drink and be merry' slogan and every third person wearing a hat that reads 'gin-gle bells', it's hard not to get caught up in the idea that you can't have a good Christmas without a few bottles of festive fizz. But what about those of us who want to remember our December? Here is some advice to help you to navigate the jolly holidays.

Embrace the magic

From ice-skating to Christmas markets, there's a whole load of activities that will get you into the Christmas spirit without having to resort to spirits! When I was little, my family used to drive around looking for the best Christmas lights on people's houses, and now I continue this tradition as a sober adult.

Gift yourself

I know that spending prolonged periods of time with your family can be tough for some, but Christmas is about being with people you love. Try to embrace spending quality time together, and enjoy being present for all of it. As I like to tell my family jokingly, before I get their real gifts out: 'I haven't got you anything, my presence is your present.'

Amend your traditions

On Christmas morning, the ritual in my house used to be: wake up, have a Bucks Fizz and eat croissants. These days we do exactly the same thing but I get the alcohol-free Bucks Fizz from M&S, or mix orange juice with alcohol-free sparkling wine. It's changed nothing apart from the fact that I don't feel like I need a nap by 11 a.m.

Get gaming

If you need distractions to survive the festive season, games are great. If you've never been a games family traditionally, maybe now's the time to start. It's worth bearing in mind that being sober while playing Monopoly gives you a tactical advantage, so when your chain of hotels is raking it in, you can thank your clear head.

Remind yourself of the positives

There are *so* many benefits to being booze-free at Christmas – from actually enjoying your food and not feeling like you'll need a full-body January detox, to receiving far better presents because people don't default to buying you bottles of gin. And remember – sober girls have more chance of making Santa's nice list! And don't even get me started on how smug you'll feel on 1 January when you wake up without a hangover. REVOLUTIONARY.

Festivals

There's no better place to prove that you can still shine without wine than at a music festival. If drunken you was anything like drunken me, festivals might previously have been a place where you spent your time downing warm cider, queuing for pungent portaloos after breaking the seal, and undertaking mini-excursions to track down your long-lost sunglasses (even £2 Primark shades seem invaluable when you're intoxicated and irrational). In case you need convincing further, here follows some advice to help you navigate the minefields of festival season.

Planning is key

While it might sound like an obvious one, festivals are a prime example of events where drinking can quickly take over, with the focus becoming less about the music and more about the beer tent.

After a few drinks, my festival experience would rarely live up to how I'd imagined it would be. Before I knew it, my plan to be front and centre for the DJ I was desperate to see transformed quickly into me listening to the faint chorus of my favourite song while stuck in an hour-long queue for the bar.

Do your research beforehand: have a clear idea of who you're going to see and give yourself time to get really excited about watching them live so that you can make sure that this takes priority over getting your hands on a drink. Make an itinerary if you have to, so that you can keep on track and not allow yourself to get distracted. Tickets to gigs and concerts are expensive, so make the most of the performances.

An additional and unexpected benefit of sober festival-going? Tricep strains are a thing of the past. Now that you're sure to remember everything the next morning, holding your phone in the air to record anything and everything seems awfully redundant.

Know your own needs

The crowds at headline acts can get a little busy, which can be quite anxiety-inducing for anyone who isn't drunk enough to tolerate being shoved in multiple directions by perspiring strangers. If you're easily overwhelmed (a particularly common state of being in early sobriety), look into going to see some of the lesser-known acts – who will be performing in smaller, quieter tents – beforehand. Not only will you be able to whisk yourself off if it all gets too much, but a bonus is that you might also discover a new artist that you really love. Some of the biggest acts started out playing smaller stages, so double points if you catch them before they get a number one. You can add to your sobriety-smugness levels by frequently mentioning that you 'saw them before everyone else loved them'.

Be selective

Many festivals are music-heavy. Although there's nothing wrong with that, if you want something more manageable, opt for one that offers a little something extra. Bestival is known for its wacky fancy dress and optional roller disco, while others such as Latitude have comedy tents as well as wellness ones where you can take a yoga class or do some crafting.

If you're not keen on a baptism by fire, start with a local day-festival that is easy enough to get home from, and work your way up. By all means, you could dive right in with a four-night camping weekender at Glasto, but you'll be a braver woman than I. Fearne Cotton's Happy Place festival started in 2019 and is completely alcohol-free. Excitingly, there's a whole host of similar ones popping up in its wake.

Enlist help

There's nothing more disappointing than queuing at the festival bar for what feels like an eternity, only to realize that its only alcohol-free offering is cranberry juice (few festivals have caught on to the sober revolution). This can make it tempting to hit the fuck-it button and order the first alcoholic drink on the menu. Instead, ask your friends to grab your drink for you – you'll know what to expect, and it will also put physical distance between you and the bar to avoid any temptation. Good friends will always say yes, but if you feel like you're indebted, then offer to repay them by queuing for the food or making sure that they all make it home safely.

Feast your eyes

In my drinking days, I saw festival food trucks as solely functional – their only purpose was to soak up the alcohol I'd already consumed so that I could simply continue to drink even more. But it turns out that festivals have some pretty good grub on offer. Take time out for a proper lunch break and sit down to enjoy the options. It's worth pointing out that some trucks will even have their own soft drink selection and are therefore more likely to stock something exciting like tonic or craft soda. The last festival I went to had a pancake/milkshake truck, which essentially sent me spiralling into a sugar high for the rest of the afternoon.

Enjoy the ride

Some festivals have the added allure of Ferris wheels and roller-coasters, but you don't need to be told that excessive alcohol consumption mixed with vigorous motion never ends well. In sobriety, the fun-fair world is your oyster and it's often a good way to break up all the dancing.

Count your losses (hint: probably none!)

According to the company who manages the lost property for Reading Festival, 500–1,000 items are handed in once the festival has wound down, and event organizers have reported losses of everything from wedding rings to ninja turtle costumes.[2] Not having to replace your phone screen every six months or explain to the DVLA that you really have lost your twelfth driving licence are two of the major perks of sobriety. I can't promise you won't misplace anything ever again, but being sober will drastically reduce your chances of dropping your prized possessions in a muddy field and not being self-aware enough to notice.

Jet Setting

The entire point of a holiday is to have a break from the usual stresses of everyday life, and give you the chance to rejuvenate and unwind. Unfortunately, this seemingly obvious point was lost on me for a very long time. I thought that a holiday was a chance to drink as much as humanly possible because you didn't have to go to work and could instead feel like you might throw up on the beach rather than on your desk.

Before sobriety, I came back from every single trip feeling more frazzled and exhausted than when I'd left – even my Thai island-hopping vacay in 2014, which should have been paradise bliss, turned into a fourteen-day bender of bar-hopping and booze cruises. Here are some pointers to help you make the most of your getaway when sober.

Avoid all-inclusive holidays

The only thing more tempting than booze is free booze, so it's best to avoid all-inclusive packages. Even if you think you'll be able to make the money back from the lunch buffet alone, it really isn't worth the risk. Opt for half board or full board, if you can. Cruises are actually great for this because everything is usually included but the booze!

Join the mile-dry club

A lot of people drink on flights because they're either scared of flying or think it will help them sleep. If your reason for doing so was the former, then now is the perfect time to get some help for that flying fear. Not only do you have more disposable income to seek professional help, but being more present and level-headed means that it's also easier to be rational about the fact that you're more likely to be struck by a meteorite than you are to be in a plane crash. If it's the latter, then be prepared: invest in a good-quality neck pillow, bring a blanket, get yourself an eye mask (silk, if we're being fussy) and even pack a lavender spray to help you jet off to the land of nod without the aid of alcohol. Earplugs wouldn't go amiss either.

Investigate local options

Before my trip of a lifetime to Bali, I was convinced that I wouldn't find any kind of alcohol-free alternative to drink there. But after a five-minute google on arrival, and a wander to the nearest mini-mart, I was delighted to find out that Bintang (a brand of beer from Indonesia) do not only a 0.0 per cent ABV version but also a 0.0 per cent ABV lemon version! Yes, it would be nice if the options were easily accessible, and you didn't have to seek them out on some sort of sober treasure hunt, but trust me that you might even start to see the fun in it, and revel in the challenge to find a good option even in the most remote places.

Find a sober travel company

There's a huge choice of holiday companies out there who special-ize in alcohol-free trips and retreats. Not only are they a great way to make other sober friends but you can also rest assured that no one will be encouraging pre-10 a.m. sangria. You can even attend sober conventions abroad: She Recovers is a popular one in the sober community, and takes place in Miami. Don't mind if we do!

Make a plan and keep busy

I'm not suggesting that you make a minute-by-minute itinerary for your entire trip, but having a rough schedule or list of things you want to do and places you want to visit can help with not reverting to drinking all day because it's the most convenient thing to do. Booking a few morning excursions or tours ahead of your arrival can also be a great drinking deterrent. There's nothing more likely to put you off getting absolutely sozzled the night before than the thought of a three-hour guided walking tour, or scheduled sunrise hike.

Take advantage of being hangover-free!

On a visit to Rome for a weekend break, I turned up to the Trevi Fountain with the foolish assumption that I'd be able to get a nice picture of myself throwing a coin into the water, like the basic tourist I am. When I got there, I could barely see through the hordes of iPads, and someone almost poked my eye out with a selfie stick. I couldn't even get close enough to throw a coin, let alone have a picture taken of me doing it. On returning to my hotel, I explained my woes to the lovely concierge at our hotel and he advised that at 6 a.m. the fountain would not only be beautiful but also relatively empty.

I thought this sounded a bit ridiculous because I was still drinking at the time – 6 a.m. was bedtime, not waking-up time – but our flight home was at 9 a.m. the next morning, so I decided to venture down to the fountain at six, as he suggested. My travelling companion and I were the only people there, and there wasn't a selfie stick in sight.

The moral of this story is that by being sober, you have a strategic advantage over other tourists. If you're going anywhere remotely busy – especially one of the boozier traveller destinations – then take advantage of your lack of hangover, get up early and beat the queues to see the sights.

Choose the right travelling companions

Sometimes I think it's less about where you go and what you do as opposed to who you go with. Choose to holiday with people you know support your sobriety, respect your boundaries and understand your triggers. My first sober holiday with the girls involved copious amounts of alcohol-free Piña Coladas. In the past the priority would have been drinking all the booze and hitting all the local nightclubs, but they made so much effort to ensure we did things such as boat excursions and lovely long lunches instead.

Pack for sobriety

I'm not advocating that you use your 20kg baggage allowance to take with you every 'quit lit' book you own (though if you want to take a picture of you reading this one by the pool, I'm not going to argue!), but even packing just a couple of sober tools can help. This could mean downloading a few podcast episodes or packing a bottle of elderflower cordial. Whatever you think might help you in a tough spot, take it.

Parenting

I'll keep this one brief because I'm not a mother, but if I was, and someone who didn't have kids tried to give me advice on parenting, I'd be pretty pissed off. There are platforms out there that specifically give advice around sobriety and parenting. Love Sober (@lovesober.cic) is one that I'd highly recommend.

Sober Girl Spotlight

'Being sober is the best decision I've ever made – for myself and my children!'

Creative director, strategist and podcaster Clemmie Telford (@clemmie_telford) gave up drinking in 2019 after noticing the link between alcohol and her mental health.

> I used alcohol to help manage tricky emotions: stress, loss of identity after becoming a mum, and a confidence boost when feeling shy or overwhelmed in social situations. And although it helped with the feeling in the short term, it's the emotional equivalent of shapewear – it might appear to hide the bits you don't like, but in the end it just spills out elsewhere.

Since binning the booze, Clemmie has noticed a positive impact not only on her mental health but also on the time spent with her children and husband: 'The Special Moments: an evening of laughter on holiday or a Sunday lunch with all the family. They aren't *less* without booze, they become *more* without. Because the "sparkly" feeling has come from you rather than from alcohol.'

Clemmie thinks being sober is, without doubt, the best thing she has ever done for herself, and it just keeps getting better too!

That doesn't mean there aren't hard bits along the way. Sometimes I find myself thinking, 'Oooh, I'd love a G & T now.' Though having that thought might catch me by surprise, I try not to overthink it or beat myself up for feeling tempted. Instead, I try to actively re-frame my focus into remembering the buzz I get when I get into bed after a night out and know that there'll be no regrets the next day, only pride. No drink would ever come close to how good that feels.

The Feeling That You're the 'Sober Girl'

I can tell you, more than anyone, what it's like to be labelled as 'the sober one', and that I recognize it can be a strange and lonely place to be. People have even introduced me as 'This is Millie, she doesn't drink.' Hopefully, times will change (after all, non-smokers aren't introduced as such), but all I can say for now is remind yourself that not drinking is something you do, not something you are. There are plenty of amazing things about you, and some of them probably result from your sobriety, so try not to get disheartened. If someone introduces you in the same way, don't be afraid to correct them or tell them afterwards how it made you feel. I am a more extreme case, given that sobriety is literally my job, but sometimes with my friends and family I'll impose a 'no sober chat' so that for a few hours I can just be me without the label.

The Doubt

I once read that when you go through a relationship break-up, there's a 'rose-tinted glasses' phase when you forget all the bad things about that relationship, including the reasons you broke up. You end up romanticizing it instead. It's why so many people go back to relationships that aren't good for them. I think the same is true in sobriety when it comes to reminiscing about your drinking days, and so I've called it the 'rosé-tinted glasses' phase.

It can be hard to look back on all those drunken nights with your mates for what they really were. Instead, you recall them as hilariously amazing memories, forgetting the way that drinking truly made you feel – miserable, in my case.

I've been told about the 'play the tape forward' method a few times now and I think it's great. It basically entails replaying those drunken nights in your head as if they were movies, right until the very end. When you look at that photo of you and your friends busting moves on the dance floor or squished into a photo booth, you might think about how happy you look, but play the tape to the end. Remember how the night ended (if you even can) and how horrific you felt the next morning.

It's important not to romanticize the drunken nights with your friends in order to stop you falling back into a doomed relationship with booze. If it's something you might find helpful, I find that observing a night out with your friends until the very end when you're sober can be like a live viewing of this tape. Last year I went for a bottomless brunch for my friend's birthday and felt slightly melancholic when everyone clinked their prosecco glasses and that chatty buzz of excitement began to build. But five hours later, after two of them had cried and one had declared she needed to vomit, my melancholy turned to relief that I was blissfully tear- and puke-free.

The Setbacks

Let me squeeze in one last cliché, because sobriety is a way of travel, it is *not* a destination. There is no 'end point' to sobriety – you don't reach sober nirvana and that's that. Even if you've made the decision to be an alcohol-free human for ever, you will still have testing days, you will still have days when you want to hit that fuck-it button and you might even have days when you do.

This is one of the reasons I don't relish the idea of counting your sober days. While I think it's great to share inspiring milestones, and for you to see how far you've come, I don't think it's good to obsess over them or that it's a fair assessment of your resolve that if you have a wobble you go straight back to zero. If you manage forty days sober and then you drink once, you don't have zero days under your belt, you have forty minus one. Every one of those days still counts for something – they still taught you lessons and they still give you a chance to evaluate what went right and what went wrong. Everything is a learning curve, and any shame or guilt that follows a slip-up is unhelpful. Don't spend your life counting the days, spend it making the days count.

I once read that if you meditate every day but miss one day and then feel terrible about not doing it, you're doing it wrong. The same goes for sobriety, because being alcohol-free is about leading a wonderful abundant life free from guilt or shame, something you can't do if you're constantly beating yourself up for not being perfect.

For some people, sobriety is a constant push-and-pull journey; it's not linear. Some weeks you will feel so strong in your sobriety that it feels like a superpower, but there will be other weeks when it will feel like a weight. If it becomes too heavy to bear and you find yourself experiencing a setback, all you need to do is work out what went wrong and use that to make sure it doesn't happen again.

The Hard Times

As much as alcohol is interwoven with our celebrations, it's equally embedded in the rituals of our commiserations too. We've already mentioned how drink is associated with romantic loss, but it is also wrapped up in physical loss of life too. From raising a toast to our loved and lost ones with their favourite tipple to using booze as a way to numb our grief, alcohol really does make an appearance during most milestones in our lives.

When I first started researching the topic for this book, I actually found more information on how to get through a sober date than I did for how to manage a period of sober grief. Perhaps that says a lot about how we're much happier to talk about our social relationship with alcohol than our emotional one.

During my research I stumbled across the Grief Network, a community run by and for bereaved young people. I emailed their founder to ask if they had any insights into the subjects of alcohol, sobriety and grief.

Rachel Wilson started the Grief Network in 2018 when she lost her mum, because she couldn't find support tailored towards young millennials dealing with grief, and it now holds regular meetings and events. In a strange way, there are parallels with why I started SGS, which shows that sometimes, when you're looking for something and can't find it, perhaps it might be your calling to create it. Perhaps it's a way to use your pain around a certain subject to help others. Rachel beautifully answered lots of my questions, so I'm going to leave you with some of her key points.

The first thing to bear in mind with grief is that a lot of people will rely on coping mechanisms they've always relied on. 'For want of a better phrase – those coping mechanisms are on steroids with grief,' Rachel told me.

So if you've turned to booze a lot when you're low, you're likely to do that. If you're someone who clams up and internalizes, you're going to do that so much more. And if you're hyper-active and productive, you go into overdrive trying to 'fix' things. With any of those mechanisms, they can eventually become ways of avoiding or distracting from processing grief.

Rachel was very clear that she doesn't like to categorize any grief coping mechanisms as 'good' or 'bad', because there is no right way to grieve. 'If you're getting through the day, you're doing a good job,' she said.

According to Rachel, grief is physical too, and sometimes you have to sit and expel the emotion: 'Whether it's through body-racking sobs, screaming into or punching a pillow, going for a run, or dancing all night, you have to allow those emotions to move through you.' She acknowledged this is much easier said than done and is always an evolving process.

There's going to be an element of doing that for the rest of your life (which is why it's so overwhelming to lose someone when you're twenty, for example – you think, 'Fuck, I have to cope with this for the next sixty-ish years'). But actively grieving is something you have to try to do, as uncomfort-able and painful as it is, because actually you do feel better afterwards.

Rachel likened grieving to exercising, because it's not necessar-ily fun in the moment, but afterwards you feel a sense of release: 'If you're blanketing that process with drinking or other avoid-ant behaviours, you're just bottling it up. It will always come out some way down the line (and it will be *far* more painful then), so it's always better to try to face it sooner rather than later.'

She told me that humans are built to grieve in the same way

that we're built to give birth or die, which is a perspective I've never really considered.

> Grieving comes often with mental health problems or other problems, but it's not a problem in and of itself, and it can't be 'fixed' or 'solved', the way you can't 'fix' whether you love someone or not. It's just an incredibly human process and response – in some moments, it's almost quite awe-inspiring, because it can feel like it exists even beyond you, because there are questions you just can't answer.

Rachel explained that it's important to remember that your body is built to grieve, so even when you feel like you're breaking, you won't.

> You'll adapt, as long and as drawn out as that process is. You'll heal, if you allow yourself to feel what you're feeling. Your brain tends to process it in waves, because you know you can't process it all at once, so you have to let those waves happen and have trust that your body and brain basically know what they're doing.

I asked Rachel if she had any tips or advice for how someone could deal with loss instead of turning to alcohol.

> Physical movement. Really, what you're trying to do with alcohol, for example, is numb yourself or anaesthetize. But there are other ways that are more effective – crying, dancing, running. It sounds preachy sometimes to say 'exercise', because I think people sometimes respond to it almost as an identity ('I'm not one of those yoga-loving, vegan,

morning people ... That's just not how I deal with things . . .'). But it's not about that, it's about you and your way of coping. So moving is great, even if that's dancing until you drop with your friends or vigorously cleaning your home.

I'm with Rachel on this one. I've never run more than 5K – and that was because it was for charity – but even walking my dog gets me out of a funk. Rachel also suggests writing, journaling and talking to people.

She also explained that support exists in constellations or in pillars. 'It's not just one thing that will help, it's a whole system of support. We have such a stifled grief culture, but you have to fight that.' She notes the importance of connection too and encourages attending meetings like those run by the Grief Network.

Being able to share your experiences and have them affirmed by other people who know what it's like is really helpful and it stops you from feeling like you're alone or you're isolated. There's something really powerful about even being able to see the number of other people who've been through it, even if you don't speak about grief at all. Being in the company of someone who understands really assuages, I think, the resentment and isolation that this happened to you too young, or that person was taken away too soon.

A lot of Rachel's advice has parallels to the advice in this book, from the importance of exercise to speaking to people who 'get it'. Though absolutely not comparable to the passing of a loved one, in a way sobriety can feel like a loss, and speaking to people who know what this particular loss feels like can be incredibly powerful. I also believe, like Rachel, that support comes in constellations and that support for your sobriety doesn't take just one shape.

I know from experience that the times when grief tends to be heightened, such as Christmas or weddings, tend to be the times when booze is more prevalent too. I asked Rachel if she agreed and had any tips for dealing with grief at those big milestone events. She agreed that 'the knees-up culture doesn't help, particularly if you've registered, "This is a hard time for me, I actually probably shouldn't drown myself in prosecco."'

> If you can try to plan ahead for it, I would do that, and don't chalk it up to succeeding or failing. The social pressure mixed with missing that person so much more at those times of year really does create a toxic tension, I think. But reach out to friends you do feel you can talk to and say, 'Hey, I need help,' or, 'This party's going to be hard for me.' There's no reason you should feel happy at that time, so try not to beat yourself up if you're not having as much fun as everyone else seems to be. It does suck a bit, because you do feel like, 'Oh, I wish I was having fun, this is a celebratory time,' but I think over time those periods get easier and you can start to see the joy in them, while also remembering and honouring that person's memory.

I realize that goes a lot for sobriety too. At parties these days, accepting the fact that I'm probably not always going to be the life and soul of the party often takes the pressure off me to feel like I should be having fun, and then more often than not I actually do end up enjoying myself.

When it comes to parting words of wisdom on grief, Rachel said, 'The main thing is to be wary of judging yourself – you've been through hell, and putting one foot in front of the other despite that is already a huge fucking achievement.'

Sober Girl Gains

- [ ] Less need for stinky portaloos
- [ ] A whole host of new drinks to test
- [ ] Tourist perks and hangover-free holidays
- [ ] A more effective way to process your feelings
- [ ] An incredible accomplishment!

10

Viva La Sober Revolución

Unleashing your inner activist

When I first stopped drinking, I felt as if I'd stumbled upon a life raft after years of being stranded unhappily on Booze Island. It was as if I'd finally returned home, to the place I was always meant to be. After a few months of revelling in my lucky escape, I started to feel guilty about the people who were still on the island; the ones I'd left behind and frantically paddled away from. People who, like me, had gone there after being sold the dream of a stress-free paradise but who had quickly realized that it was actually a glorified dump surrounded by hangover-infested waters. People who had come to realize that getting off the island wasn't half as easy as it had been to get on.

I thought about the people who were desperate to come home and about how I could warn those who might be deciding to visit about the realities and potential dangers of alcohol.

I thought, and still think, about them daily. Apparently, this guilt isn't uncommon, and sobriety is often thought to be accompanied by a renewed sense of purpose, usually one that involves a desire to shake up the system that kept us drinking. When you're no longer imbibing, you realize not only how ever-present booze is, but also the subtle ways it infiltrates our daily lives.

Perhaps the most important point before we start this chapter in detail is that activism around alcohol is *not* about banning it. After the last prohibition (a nationwide ban on the production, importation and sale of alcoholic beverages) resulted in a significant number of deaths caused by the production of illegal homemade concoctions such as bathtub gin, a ban on alcohol would be a less than ideal scenario. Plus, I'm absolutely not here to dictate what people can and can't consume. Some people are, after all, perfectly happy to stay on Booze Island.

It's not about trying to coerce anyone into sobriety either, or tutting disapprovingly at anyone who dares to order a glass of wine. It's not about taking away anyone's right or choice to drink, but it *is* about advocating for harm reduction; changing the stories we tell ourselves about the role that booze plays in our lives; and challenging narratives that sell alcohol as 'mummy juice', 'lady petrol', or an essential part of being a woman. It's about understanding that alcohol harm affects society as a whole, even if it doesn't affect you directly.

Finally, it's about accepting that the picture is bigger than just you and me, and acknowledging our privileges when it comes to the support we receive for sobriety. Practically, this looks like advocating for affordable treatment for those who aren't in a financial position to seek professional help, and campaigning for the alcohol industry to stop exploiting minority and oppressed groups through aggressively targeted marketing.

In this last chapter I'll be going into what I like to think of as 'the work': the change-making and the activism opportunities pertaining to alcohol. This includes everything above, as well as understanding how we can encourage the bars in our local area to be more sober inclusive by stocking a greater selection of alcohol-free options, and trying to untangle the link between alcohol and feminism. It means talking about how alcohol is marketed, what the charities in this space are doing, and how you can get involved.

These conversations are already happening, but not enough people are giving them a wider platform. As a result, many are failing to gather momentum and pick up the support they need in order for change to happen. This chapter barely scratches the surface, and I recognize that more issues need addressing than the ones I've been able to fit in. Fortunately, the work continues well beyond the pages of this book.

If you're in early sobriety or just starting a journey of sober curiosity, perhaps you might want to flick forward to my final note on page 275 instead, and come back to this chapter later on. For now, you've learned pretty much everything I know about how to navigate an alcohol-free lifestyle. If we end our journey here, please keep in touch, please come to a meet-up or please drop a friendly direct message into my inbox. If you're sticking around for the rest of this chapter, it's time to get your change-maker hat on and pull out your notepad. Let's get down to business – there's a lot of work to be done.

Sober Girl Spotlight

'Sobriety made me want to go out and change the world for the better!'

Meg Ellis (@megellisuk) gave up drinking in 2018, after struggling with alcohol for most of her twenties: 'I ended up in lots of negative situations as a result of my drinking. In my early twenties I even tripped and forward-rolled down the steps outside Wembley Park station, and ended up having my head stitched together. I was told I was lucky to be alive!'

Meg had been working in talent management in London, but decided to leave to explore Asia, and it was there, at twenty-eight, that she set herself a challenge – 'a year to change her life'. Upon returning home to Newcastle, she ended up taking a morning cleaning job and evening pub work to fund her first business. However, as she tried to balance the early mornings and late nights, she realized that she couldn't cope with the unproductivity of her drinking any more.

Within two weeks of giving up alcohol, Meg became the founding member – with fellow activist Jameela Jamil – of diversity and inclusion platform iWeigh. Shortly after, she also became a representative for Chamber of Commerce North East Business. Consequently, in 2020 Meg was awarded a Northern Power Women Futures Award. Meg changed her life with sobriety, but if she hadn't stopped drinking, a platform like iWeigh – which has helped so many people – might not be the success it is today. 'Quitting alcohol taught me compassion, and my learning and productivity have sky-rocketed. Activism allows me to be part of something bigger, and has given me the confidence to use my voice and advocate for others.' Meg is now working in her dream role as a talent director but spends her spare time volunteering in her local community.

Big Alcohol

Everyone has a friend who is an FBI-level internet detective, and in my friendship group that person is me. Once I started to research the alcohol industry, I seemed to pull at a thread that continued to unravel. After finding myself deep in the depths of internet conspiracies and mysteries surrounding 'Big Alcohol' (the producers, distributors, retailers and marketers of alcohol products), I decided to enlist the help of someone with far more knowledge of the subject than me to give us the full picture we need before we can understand how to create change.

Richard Piper is CEO of one of the UK's leading alcohol charities, Alcohol Change UK. Formed from the 2017 merger of Alcohol Concern and Alcohol Research UK, Alcohol Change UK is known for its flagship programmes Alcohol Awareness Week and Dry January. I contacted Richard on Twitter, where his bio declares that he is 'not anti-alcohol, just anti-alcohol-harm', and so I started by asking him what he means by this.

Richard explained that when members of the public hear the name Alcohol Change UK, they correctly assume that it is an alcohol charity, but often they incorrectly assume that this means the charity is anti-alcohol. As we know, people can be very defensive about their alcohol consumption and resist anyone trying to take it away. He explained that people also like to revert to simple binaries – surely you can only be either for or against alcohol? Given Alcohol Change UK is a charity, people often assume it falls into the latter group.

'This all happens in [people's] heads in a micro-second,' he went on. 'So we make it clear, up front, as fast as we can – and repeat it – that we are not against alcohol but are against the harm from alcohol.'

Richard also explained that a lot of people won't have heard of 'alcohol harm' because it's a bit of jargon, but it's essential that we introduce this concept quickly and distinguish it from alcohol.

Like me, Richard doesn't believe that eliminating alcohol from society is a realistic – or even a desirable – solution to the problems of alcohol harm. He likened this to a charity trying to stop knife crime: 'They're not against knives per se, and wouldn't want to ban knives from society, but they are against their use in a certain way. The same applies to us.' Alcohol Change UK's vision is a society in which alcohol causes no harm.

Unravelling the mysteries

One of the first things I came across in my research was the Portman Group – the body that operates the code of practice when it

comes to the naming, packaging and promotion of alcoholic drinks. Essentially, they are one of the regulators policing
the marketing and labelling of booze in the UK. But if you go a
little deeper you will discover that the Portman Group is mem-
bered and mainly funded by some of the biggest alcohol brands
in the business. This could lead to the perception that there is a
lack of independence between the regulator and the industry
itself, and criticism that those abiding by the rules are essentially
the ones who have helped to shape them. The Portman Group
does have an independent complaints panel which operates separately from the Portman Group to judge on cases brought against
alcohol producers for breach of the code. But as the Portman
Group is a non-statutory body, there remain concerns over a
potential lack of the accountability and public scrutiny that would
be found in other, non-self-regulated industries.[1]

In Richard's view, the biggest problem is that we, as citizens,
have absolutely no say over any of the above in our own country:
'That is completely unacceptable in a democracy. There must be
some form of public accountability – through government – of
alcohol marketing and labelling so that we can decide what
counts as acceptable and unacceptable, i.e. the code.' The code is
the key, he said, because the work of the panel can then be scru-
tinized against a code that has been agreed upon by the public
and not just by the alcohol industry.

I asked Richard why this self-policing is even allowed to happen and he told me that it's a big question without a logical
answer (something I hear a lot when asking questions around
alcohol). He did tell me, however, that it lies in history and politics: around questions of individual freedom; evolving cultural
and political attitudes; control of free markets; the relationship

between the state and industry; taxation; morality; criminality; and in more recent years, the growth in medical science's understanding of alcohol health harm versus a massively wealthy and globalized alcohol industry.

There is one saving grace, though. Richard explained that certain elements of labels are mandated by government: the strength in ABV; the volume of liquid; the presence of any of the fourteen 'common allergens'; and certain words that must and must not be used. The Food Standards Agency also has some jurisdiction over the products.

When I asked if all aspects of the alcohol industry are self-regulating, Richard told me that although marketing and labelling are, alcohol advertising is regulated by the Advertising Standards Authority (ASA), which is led by the advertising industry and Ofcom – which, in turn, has its duties set by Parliament, making it more independent. Licensing – what can be sold when, by whom and where – is regulated by central and local government.

I questioned if it would be easier to just have one alcohol body that regulates everything and Richard admitted he's not sure: 'It might feel neater to have one body, but the most important question is whether it would make it more effective. I think too often we see politicians make the mistake of thinking that the solution to problems is reorganizing the structures, but then leave the cultures and actual practices untouched.'

He thinks we should be asking what better regulation looks like, and although we should include restructuring as one option, we shouldn't assume up front that restructuring is the best option: 'I would argue that we need a piece of work to more clearly set out the problems with the current regulatory system and then identify solutions that we want government to put in place.'

Beyond the bottle

You'll probably be familiar with Drinkaware: they are referenced on the label of most bottles, they run alcohol education campaigns, and they are pretty much the go-to for alcohol-related advice with their 'drink responsibly' slogan. The Drinkaware website was set up in 2004 and the Drinkaware Trust in 2006 – both by the Portman Group.

Although they're now an independent body, Drinkaware is still funded by the alcohol industry, and I start to understand why Drinkaware's message is 'drink responsibly': if they're funded by the alcohol industry, it makes sense that they won't be telling us to stop drinking completely any time soon. At this point I felt like I'd opened Pandora's box, because I realized that even this messaging puts the responsibility with the drinker and not with the toxic substance. It reinforces the idea that if we can't handle our drink, it's our fault or a human flaw, rather than the fact that no one is really built to ingest ethanol.

Richard explained that Drinkaware is the industry's way of being seen as acting responsibly by giving the public information about the dangers of misusing alcohol, and trying to persuade people to drink 'safely': 'Arguably, Drinkaware itself is not terrible, but the industry could be doing more. For example, by requiring the Chief Medical Officers' guidance or health warnings to be displayed on adverts and bottles, rather than just signposting to the Drinkaware website and relying on us to go and actively seek out their information on the harms of drinking alcohol.'

Who Are the New Targets?

As an industry that isn't stringently regulated, which has a desire to ensure we keep buying its products, who are some of the most vulnerable groups when it comes to being exploited by the alcohol industry?

Women

After many years of targeting their products at men, Big Alcohol quickly realized that if they wanted to make more money, they needed to recruit more drinkers, and those drinkers needed to be female. This shift is what led the European Centre for Monitoring Alcohol Marketing (EUCAM) to publish a 2008 trends report titled 'Women – the new market', which explored the notable surge in launches of gender-targeted beverages such as light beers, low-calorie options and alcopops.[2]

Since then, the recruitment drive for more female consumers has shown no signs of slowing down, with noteworthy launches such as Strongbow's rosé cider and the female counterpart to Johnnie Walker Scotch: limited edition Jane Walker. The marketing of these products has been clever, of course. Jane Walker Scotch was launched in line with International Women's Day, and the brand pledged a dollar from every sale to women's organizations. A nice gesture, but apparently another tick in the box for reinforcing the message that drinking is a positive addition to women's liberation.

Through these smart marketing and expensive advertising campaigns, alcohol has been so expertly tied up in what it means to be a woman that many of us question whether we'll even be real women without it. From messages on greeting cards to influential celebrity endorsements, as any good marketer knows, if you want to sell a product you have to create the need for it, and for alcohol that seems to involve selling us the idea that drinking makes us powerful, confident and stylish. Without it, we are awkward, basic and boring.

The problem is, we still see drinking with our nineties' ladette glasses: it's a bold move in sticking it to the man. But every time we drink, we're simply lining the pockets of the man. Not drinking, and admitting we can't 'keep up', feels like the ultimate betrayal of feminism, but really, it's a rebellious defiance of the patriarchy.

Luckily, the hurricane of aggressive gender marketing by the alcohol industry hasn't gone unnoticed. In 2018, academics at Glasgow Caledonian University working in the field of substance misuse launched the #dontpinkmydrink campaign on social media to identify and expose examples of cynical alcohol marketing. Not only that, but the release of books such as *Quit Like a Woman* and *Drink: The Intimate Relationship Between Women and Alcohol* means that the conversation about alcohol as a feminist issue is gaining momentum. If you're wondering what's the big deal with a little pink gin or thinking that this all might be a slight overreaction to rosé-flavoured cider, it's important to know that the stats show that alcohol is not empowering women, it is killing them.

Between 1999 and 2017, alcohol-related deaths in the USA increased by 51 per cent overall, but for women that percentage increase was 85 per cent. More than that, alcohol is now the leading global risk factor for early death among people aged 15–49.[3]

As we learned in Chapter Three, even women's physiological make-up means that we have a greater risk of our health being harmed by alcohol than men do. Let's not forget that 8 per cent of breast cancer cases in the UK are thought to be caused by alcohol consumption. We might want to drink like our male counterparts, but by trying to do so we are actually risking our lives in the process.

Aside from health, alcohol is a major factor in so many of the key women's issues that currently plague our society. Despite the fact that chemicals such as GHB and Rohypnol are commonly noted as 'date-rape' drugs when used to spike women's drinks, numerous studies have shown that the most commonly used date-rape drug is, in fact, alcohol. Not only is it being used as a weapon against us in this way, but it is playing a major role in the violence experienced by so many women today. In 2016–17 in England and Wales, 35.8 per cent of perpetrators in sexual assault cases were under the influence of alcohol,[4] and when it comes to domestic violence, it is thought that anywhere between 25 and 50 per cent of perpetrators will have been drinking at the time of the assault.[5] In some studies, the figure is as high as 73 per cent, and research conducted with police officers in the North East of England found that some officers were unable to remember the last time they went to a domestic incident where alcohol was *not* involved.[6]

When I started my research for this book, I asked my followers what alcohol topics they wanted to see more discussion around, and I was flooded with messages urging me to talk about sexual and domestic violence. To ensure there's an expert voice at the centre of all this, I reached out to Kristina Sperkova again. She explained that one of the first things to note is that when people do something under the influence of alcohol, the unacceptable becomes accepted, tolerated and excused – but only if you are the perpetrator: 'If the victim has been intoxicated, it is seen as her fault and alcohol is, all of a sudden, not an excuse but a reason for punishment.'

Kristina went on to say that women's-rights defenders are, of course, aware of this injustice. It's why they refuse to discuss alcohol's role, because it is a distracting element that takes attention from the real reason for the sexual assault: the perpetrator. 'This conversation matters for the victims: we need this conversation about the real effects and harm of alcohol, and the myths, to help end victim-blaming, victim-shaming and the victims blaming themselves.' Kristina also mentioned that a considerable number of sexual assault victims are using alcohol to self-medicate, and that they are 2.3 times more likely to go on to develop an alcohol-use disorder.

Kristina explained that the answer is wrapped up in alcohol policy, norms and discourse: 'We can use population-level alcohol-policy measures that lead to a decrease in violence and crime in general – higher alcohol price, lower alcohol availability, and much less alcohol marketing, including sexualizing and objectifying alcohol adverts.'

According to Kristina, these measures can result in reduced alcohol use and, in turn, help to prevent alcohol-related sexual assault. She believes they have the power to change alcohol norms over time because they are cost-effective, scientifically proven and a highly impactful solution. Most importantly, because they are not talking about any specific group, no one is (or should be) blamed or victimized. Kristina said that these issues are two examples that clearly show that everyone benefits from alcohol policy-making: the alcohol users and the non-users alike. Everyone benefits from sexual assault and domestic violence being eliminated.

The LGBTQIA+ Community

Unsurprisingly, the exploitation of certain groups by the alcohol industry doesn't end with women, and booze brands have been quick to capitalize on the mounting acceptance of sexual and gender minorities too.

Over the past few decades, the alcohol industry has made numerous successful attempts to appeal to the LGBTQIA+ community by using the ever-growing shift towards true equality as a lucrative marketing opportunity. Their tactics have included everything from releasing rainbow edition products to sponsoring Pride events.

There's no denying that big brands partnering with LGBTQIA+ causes can, in some respects, have a positive impact. First, it amplifies messages to those who might not otherwise hear them, bringing awareness of important causes, and second, the financial support of these brands — via sponsorship or product percentage donations – can go towards raising vital funds for tackling issues within the community. But here's the problem – what if one of those issues is being caused by the very product offering the financial support that could be used to tackle it?

Substance abuse is particularly high in LGBTQIA+ communities, and a report produced by Stonewall claimed that one in six LGBTQIA+ identifiers drinks almost daily.[7] Add to that the fact that a University of Cardiff study showed that alcohol can make people more racist and homophobic – given that it acts as a catalyst for people expressing their prejudices in the form of violent hate crime – and you can see why there might be a conflict of interest.[8]

Scott Pearson is the founder of Proud and Sober, and one of the hosts for the sober meet-up group Queers Without Beers. (He also happens to be the first-ever sober friend I made.) Over the years, Scott has taught me a lot about why addiction is so prevalent in the LGBTQIA+ communities, and a lot of the reasons are tied up in shame and self-medication. He always recommends Matthew Todd's book *Straight Jacket* for eye-opening reading on this subject.

From Scott's perspective, the partnerships between alcohol and Pride do more harm than good.

> One of the main problems is that attendees are subliminally fed messages to associate being LGBTQIA+ with being boozy from day one, and speaking from my own experience, the reason I didn't give up drinking sooner was because alcohol is now so tied up in this culture that I was fearful I'd lose my friends and would no longer fit in.

Scott says that thankfully he realized sobriety was the right thing for him and did it anyway, but he still worries that for young people, and for those who only have the scene as a place to feel their most comfortable, it might not be the same.

Scott also thinks that more recently booze brand sponsorships are overshadowing the true meaning of Pride, with the focus for many becoming drinking and not the celebration itself.

Alcohol has become so synonymous with celebration that we've forgotten what it's like to truly celebrate something and feel it at the same time. Pride should be about celebrating defiance and differences, *not* drunkenness. Sure, alcohol brands might have chucked a lot of money to help fund the celebrations but they definitely don't sponsor my pride.

The Black community

Statistically speaking, Black people drink less than their Caucasian counterparts, but it seems that the alcohol industry knows this, because over the past few decades they have consistently tried to target Black communities in order to recruit new drinkers and generate more profit.

Studies in the US have investigated and proven the disproportionate number of alcohol billboards and transport adverts in Black neighbourhoods. In 2004, alcohol advertising appeared during all fifteen of the television programmes most watched by African American youth (the industry spent just under $5 million to buy commercial time on these programmes) and Black Entertainment Television (a cable television network that targets the Black community) was the number one outlet for overall alcohol spending in 2003–04.[9]

To add insult to injury, black people may also be more likely to face legal consequences when drinking in public than other races, simply because of their skin colour.

Kirstin Walker is the founder of Sober Brown Girls, a community for sober and sober-curious women of colour. Kirstin stopped drinking after realizing that she was in a toxic (pun intended) relationship with wine, and founded SBG shortly after, when she noticed the lack of Black women who were openly talking about their sobriety online: 'Now don't get me wrong, some amazing women and groups are out there, but I just wanted to be one more voice, one more face. People have to know Black women recover too!'

Kirstin is based in the US and I asked for her thoughts on the stats about Big Alcohol targeting the Black community.

I think it's troubling. If you go into any urban community, you still see a liquor store on most corners. The oppressed are systematically being drugged and there is so little education in the Black community about the effects of alcohol. It's heartbreaking to watch the poisoning of a society. The poorest community might lack a proper playground for their young ones, but you'd better believe the liquor store is in plain sight.

Evidence suggests that in much the same way as those in the LGBTQIA+ community, Black people might struggle more with substance abuse because of social stigma, discrimination and the violence they may suffer, or live in fear of suffering – all of which can heighten anxiety, depression, and sometimes lead to self-medication with alcohol.

I asked Kirstin if she thinks social stigma and the pressures of being a Black woman influenced her drinking.

I think Black womanhood is beautiful! I love who I am. Unfortunately, the fact remains that we are the most under-protected part of society. As Black women, we carry so much on our

shoulders – we are stressed, we are weighed down, we want
relief, and many turn to alcohol as a release.

Speaking for herself, she said alcohol was the easiest way to numb
herself and get a break from it all.

There is evidence to suggest that race might be a factor to consider in relation to the negative impacts of alcohol. Remember the
old 'red wine is good for you' research? The studies that showed
a link between moderate drinking and a lowered risk of Type
2 diabetes, heart disease and premature mortality (don't forget
your other elevated risks, such as cancer, outweigh these!) were
conducted among mostly white populations, and now some studies have suggested that Black people may not experience similar
risk reduction.[10]

I pointed out to Kirstin that this feels unjust because Black
communities might not be aware that they could be at a greater
risk from the negative impacts of alcohol, and she agreed that we
need more research findings like this published in the mainstream media. 'The impact of alcohol isn't just one size fits all,'
she said. 'Gender, age and life circumstances are always brought
to the forefront of alcohol research, but race matters too!'

She told me that one of the problems a lot of Black women face
is that speaking about alcohol problems can still very much come
with a stigma.

The Black community is very open talking about high blood
pressure, cholesterol, diabetes and cancer, but bringing up
mental health or us recognizing we have a problematic relationship with alcohol can sometimes make the room uncomfortable.
Alcohol is just not seen as the drug it really is.

In her family, topics such as depression, anxiety or suicide were never talked about. 'Because it was so taboo, I felt so alone,' she explained. 'The problem is, when we keep issues private we perpetuate shame and secrecy.' She believes it's so important for more Black men and women to speak openly about addiction and sobriety to inspire others. Most importantly, more Black, sober voices need to be given a platform: 'Let us tell our stories. Representation matters and we connect to what is relatable.'

Starting Sober Brown Girls felt like the closest thing Kirstin could do to open her window and scream to the world, 'I've got a problem with alcohol, and I'm quitting.' So I ask her what she'd yell out of her window to any Black women who are considering sobriety or questioning their relationships with alcohol. Her words of advice were: 'There is no need to be ashamed and you're so not alone. The face of sobriety includes you too! There is a sisterhood of support that is ready with open arms to take you in. The other side is beautiful and you deserve this healing.'

The wider repercussions

Once you start looking into it, you soon realize that the alcohol industry has a lot of money at its disposal to make sure everyone they want to buys their products. One of the main problems is that while alcohol addiction is indiscriminate, affecting everyone from the rich and famous to those in third-world countries, it can have larger consequences for its poorer victims due to the expenses involved in its treatment. In some communities, it doesn't help that addiction is criminalized rather than seen as something where help and intervention are desperately needed.

It seems as though pretty much every community or culture

has been heavily targeted at some point, and I would need more than one chapter to explore every injustice.

When the alcohol industry realized the Latinx community was one of the fastest-growing populations, they aggressively targeted it. In much the same way that Pride celebrations have been commandeered by alcohol brands, cultural holidays such as Cinco de Mayo have been similarly co-opted. In 2006, Anheuser-Busch (who produce brands such as Budweiser) budgeted $60 million for ads in the Latinx media in the US,[11] but thankfully this commercialization of Cinco de Mayo has not gone unnoticed, and activists have waged various campaigns against the alcohol industry for promoting negative stereotypes and alcohol abuse within the Latinx community.

Other demographics in the firing line include adolescents, sports fans, mums, dieters, vegans, coeliacs, students, young professionals and older men. Trust me, if you are a living, breathing human being the alcohol industry is looking at how it can convince you to drink. No one is spared.

Profit over people

According to the Institute of Economic Affairs, the revenue generated from alcohol taxes in the UK is over £10 billion.[12] Could it be that perhaps this staggering figure is the reason the government doesn't seem to be in too much of a hurry to change the system?

'If you're asking whether governments are attracted – sometimes even seduced – by that taxation, then I think the answer is probably yes,' Richard from Alcohol Change UK told me. He went on to explain that this doesn't mean that governments don't care about the human harm and misery. However, he does think governments appear to want to remain ignorant about this harm and seem to have a perception bias against seeing it as something that they can and should tackle.

I asked Richard whether it's a fair assessment to say that the truth is being kept from us, but he doesn't think so. 'I wouldn't say that the truth is actually hidden from people,' he said. 'All the research is published in journals, the Chief Medical Officers' guidance is available online, and the major 2015 PHE report into alcohol harm is available online.'

If that's the case, why do hardly any of us know about the real harms of alcohol? Richard thinks that the problem isn't necessarily with transparency but with communication. He believes that the Chief Medical Officers' guidance should be printed on every bottle of alcohol and every advert selling it, and information about the harms of drinking should be on there too. 'The alcohol industry is working endlessly to stop this happening, and has been winning,' he warned. 'But we are taking them on.'

People should be shocked, sad, angry – but also motivated. He told me, 'Alcohol harm *is* avoidable, change is possible, and we can make it happen.'

Be the Change

As you will have now realized, the alcohol industry is a very powerful one, with a lot of money to throw around, so trying to change the way the world thinks about drinking so that we can reduce the harms of alcohol does officially make us the underdog. The good news is that there's no such thing as too small when it comes to activism – the change can start with me or you.

Richard thinks there are five main things we need to implement to reduce the harms of alcohol.

Better knowledge

There's still lots we don't know about why alcohol harm affects certain people and groups more than others, and, most importantly, about the best ways to reduce it. Alcohol Change UK is funding promising new research and communicating that research to the public and the government in a direct and accessible way, ensuring that everyone is as well informed as possible.

Better policy and regulation

Minimum Unit Pricing (which stops dirt-cheap alcohol being sold) would make a big difference, as would increasing alcohol duty every year at 2 per cent above inflation, and public control over labelling and marketing rules. Scotland has already introduced Minimum Unit Pricing to great effect.

Cultural change

Making workplace cultures more inclusive for non-drinkers and better at supporting people with drinking problems would be a hugely beneficial shift. This means making it socially and culturally normal to say that you've had a drinking problem; no longer having to put up with #sobershaming; people no longer asking why someone else isn't drinking; demystifying drinking problems; and removing the shame and stigma.

Individual behaviour change

We need people to make empowered choices when it comes to taking control of their drinking and participating in campaigns such as Dry January and Sober Spring.

Supporting alcohol treatment

All treatment types have to be more effective, more client-centric and properly funded, with much better early identification and advice, including social prescribing (when health professionals refer patients to support in the community, in order to improve their health and wellbeing).

Though some things are best left to the professionals, here are some ideas for action you can take to promote and inspire change within your own community.

Sign up

If you head to the Tools section on the Sober Girl Society website (sobergirlsociety.com), you'll find loads more information on unleashing your inner activist, including how you can sign up to be a campaigner with Alcohol Change UK. Following your sign-up, you'll receive regular email blasts full of concrete action that you can take to prevent alcohol harm in your community, including fundraising ideas or suggestions for letters that you can write to your local MP.

Support sustainability

In my opinion, mindful drinking shouldn't be limited to the volume of alcohol you're consuming, it should also encompass making more conscious choices when it comes to sustainability. There are a number of ways that alcohol production can negatively impact the planet. For starters, the manufacturing process uses a lot of ingredients which require a significant amount of water, land use and machinery. Seeing as we don't need alcohol to survive, these resources could be better used to provide food aid for those who need it.

There is also the issue of packaging: the 2020 report from drinks company C&C Group states that only 50 per cent of glass containers are currently recycled within the industry.[13] Bars and restaurants are responsible for sending 200,000 tonnes of glass to landfill each year, and that's not to mention all the plastic and cardboard too.

The C&C report also states that transportation of raw materials and finished goods can increase a company's carbon footprint, and some of that transportation is pretty expensive – for example, tequila can only be produced in Mexico but is sold all over the world, and champagne can only be made in, well, Champagne.

As well as the carbon footprint from transportation, packaging and waste, the processing of fruits and grains and complex distilling requires a good deal of energy – for the heating and cooling of stills and so on.

Research in the report confirms that each year alcohol manufacturers in the United States release a quantity of greenhouse gases equivalent to the emissions of 1.9 million average US households.

♥ Obviously, reducing your alcohol consumption is the easiest way to help, but you can also do your bit if or when you do drink by opting for more sustainable booze brands. More recently, some packs of canned beer have ditched plastic pack rings in favour of new glue technology, or you could choose glass that you know will be recycled.

♥ You can campaign on sites like change.org for booze brands to adopt more sustainable practices.

♥ Bear in mind that even non-alcoholic drinks require some of the same manufacturing processes detailed above, so even if you're sober it's still great to make more sustainable choices where you can!

Campaign for sober inclusivity

One of the biggest but easiest things that we can do to help reduce alcohol harm is making sure that those who are sober, drinking mindfully or just wanting to take a break from booze are well supported. This means ensuring that social spaces are as alcohol-free-friendly as possible. Here's how we do it . . .

♥ *Workplaces*

If the only alcohol-free drink at the office Christmas party is orange juice, and team-building activities don't extend beyond after-work wine, then it's easy to feel discouraged with your decision not to imbibe. Luckily, lots of bigger companies now have diversity and inclusion committees, so it's important to make the most of them. After all, their aim is to ensure colleagues feel included and supported at work.

Failing that, you should at least have an HR team or a manager, so speaking to them about your concerns is important. Express that you would still like to be involved in social activities because you recognize they're an important way to bond with your colleagues, but that you'd love to see more ways of accommodating those who don't wish to drink.

If your place of work has a particularly boozy culture, perhaps you could suggest ways it could be changed. Maybe the last Friday of the month could be an alcohol-free bar? Could the next team outing be more activity-based, where the sole focus isn't on drinking? You could also suggest bringing in an independent company to give a work-based talk on mindful drinking. Workplaces these days know that creating a good culture is important for their business, so should be willing to accommodate – or at least listen to – your suggestions.

♥ *Pubs, bars and restaurants*
Places where drinking is the main focus can be difficult to navigate when you're sober. I've given you my best tips on menu-scanning and secret, behind-the-bar ordering, but what happens when you don't come up trumps? Making food and drink establishments aware that they're potentially losing customers through their lack of offering is important for people like us, but it's also equally important for the businesses themselves.

The pub trade is quieter than ever, having experienced a decline in customers that is thought to be, in part, to do with the growth of more conscious drinking. Having these conversations with your local could actually be doing them a massive favour. Start by explaining how you might be more likely to visit if there were more choice, and perhaps even suggest some of your favourite alcohol-free beverages for them to look into.

It's also worth pointing out that they'd make more money from you as a non-drinker if they could charge you for two non-alcoholic beers rather than a couple of Diet Cokes from the pump – this logic usually sells it!

Richard from Alcohol Change UK suggests offering to meet the owner for a productive discussion – and proposing to put the pub/restaurant on a local list of alcohol-free-friendly establishments in order to drive customers to them.

Clubsodaguide.com, run by Club Soda, is the UK's first directory for low- and no-alcohol drinks, and the best places to find them. The guide rates pubs and bars on how friendly they are for mindful drinkers, and you can even purchase a Soberhack Pack which includes anonymous cards you can leave behind for venues. They say things like, 'Thank you for being a great place for mindful drinkers' or 'Times are changing, we would have loved it if you had a few more alcohol-free drinks available.' Both cards point to the Club Soda Guide website, which includes advice for venues on how they can become a great place for mindful drinkers. If you're outside of the UK, you could simply make your own!

♥ *Anywhere else that sells booze!*

Aeroplanes, festivals, theatres, concert venues, hotels, sporting venues . . . You name it, they could all be a little more sober inclusive. Take bridal shops, for instance, which offer the bride-to-be a glass of champagne as she picks *the* dress. If you don't drink, there's rarely an alternative on offer, and you might leave the store feeling less special than you'd imagined.

Everyone deserves to feel like they're being taken into account and catered for, especially if they've spent a lot of money on something like tickets to a gig, a flight or the dress of their dreams. Writing a letter/email or reaching out to venues on social media are easy ways of doing this, and again, appealing to their business sense always works.

If, for instance, I went to a hotel and their only alcohol-free option was Coke, I'd explain that I'd be less likely to stay there again, and with a growing population of teetotallers, I'm sure other people would feel the same. If your alcohol-free experience isn't satisfactory, let establishments and companies know. Even if you have no intention ever to visit again, they might implement changes that could help someone else in the future.

Question booze-themed buys

From mulled-wine toilet roll to pink champagne face masks, unnecessary booze buys are everywhere. Unless you really want your nether regions to smell like cloves and star anise, I think we're sensible enough to realize that it's all a marketing ploy designed to make you spend a little bit more than you normally would on a packet of value bog roll.

It's not just the flavoured or infused merchandise, alcohol slogans are everywhere. Finding a Valentine's card that doesn't include a sentiment that vaguely likens your significant other to the gin to your tonic is near impossible, and while none of these products are dangerous (I'm sure a lot of people will be quick to defend them as a bit of harmless fun) I do think it's important to consider the wider narrative they reinforce in society.

What worries me is the casual way that we normalize alcohol, the way we forget it's a drug that kills thousands of people. Instead, we add it to crisp flavours and buttercream frosting. These products relay the message that we need booze to make it through any sort of struggle or period of anxiety; that good wine is as important as good relationships; that we can't dance unless drunk; that Christmas isn't fun without festive fizz. They also normalize drinking to younger people as something 'cool', show-ing alcohol consumption as a 'grown up' thing to do and cementing it as behaviour to be idolized and imitated. We have to be more mindful about what we're promoting and the stories we're telling. How can we tackle it?

- ♥ Campaign for tighter regulations on the places these products can be sold – i.e. away from children, not in gift shops, and so on.

- ♥ Campaign for health warnings to feature on these products' packaging – perhaps greetings cards need to come with an alcohol warning or a reminder about recommended weekly unit intake on the back.

- ♥ Encourage shops to expand their offering and shine a light on being booze-free. I'd buy a sobrie-tea mug for sure!

Give money

Alcohol Change UK is clear that they do not and will not receive funding from alcohol companies, which means a lot of the work they, and other alcohol charities, carry out relies on donations. Alcohol Change UK is currently running a big deficit, and they need to turn that around in order to stay afloat and keep their brilliant work going – so perhaps consider hosting a fundraiser or using Facebook's birthday donation feature to help raise funds for the people doing amazing work in this field.

Use your social influence

I've noticed a recent surge of both influencers and celebrities on Instagram partnering with some of the big booze brands. In 2019, pop star Rita Ora came under fire for glamorizing drinking to some of her underage following, declaring that the tequila brand she was working with 'highlights strong independent women'.[14]

The problem here is that while the ASA (Advertising Standards Authority) regulates UK advertising on Instagram – with a few rules, including that those appearing in the adverts must look at least twenty-five, and alcohol can't be linked with sexual activity – there really isn't anything to stop a celebrity from posing with a glass (or even bottles) of wine in an unsponsored post.

What's more, most people don't even need to be paid these days to show off their booze habit. As Holly Whitaker puts it in her book *Quit Like a Woman*, 'The ace up Big Alcohol's sleeve is now a woman with an Instagram account.' We have become our own marketers of booze and Big Alcohol is reaping the benefits in their profits.

When you start to notice messages, particularly on social media, that provide misinformation about booze or continue to peddle incorrect narratives (wine being the perfect method of self-care, gin glasses emblazoned with the words 'mama fuel', and so on), your gut reaction might be to fire off an angry missive, but there are a few simple steps you can follow to ensure that you put your message across in a calm and sophisticated manner.

♥ Keep in mind that there is a very stark difference between cancel culture and education. Cancel culture is declaring a person or brand is officially 'over' for their views on a certain subject. Education, on the other hand, is taking the time to realize that not everyone has the knowledge about certain subjects that you do, and that there is a way of politely prompting people and brands without trying to demonize a person or a business as a whole.

♥ Be very clear on why a post is problematic, and be sure to explain with evidence if possible. For example, it isn't OK to call out your friend who is posting about her Saturday garden cocktail creation, but it is OK to ask a brand to reconsider promoting alcohol as a coping mechanism for stress. Another example is from the brand that sells period pants and which encouraged everyone to raise a glass to a better period. There's a lot of information out there to suggest that alcohol has a detrimental effect on menstrual cycles so this is what made it problematic.

♥ Be polite (firm but fair) – there's no need for unkindness or aggression. We're all trying our best, people prompt me all the time. If you'd rather message someone directly, that's fine, but bear in mind that a lot of brands will just delete a private comment whereas a public comment usually gets more notice.

Provide resources. It's all well and good pointing something out to someone, but if you can refer them to educational materials by tagging in accounts or websites where they can learn more, even better. Here are some examples:

'I love your account and adore your usual content, but I was quite disappointed with this post about relationships and the suggestion that the most effective way to communicate with a woman is through wine. I appreciate the post has been made in good humour but there are plenty of other (and healthier) ways to communicate with a woman – especially when a lot of us don't drink at all! Some great resources are @sobergirlsociety and sobergirlsociety.com. Thank you for hearing me out!'

'I really like your page and the way you promote good mental health and self-care, but I was a little surprised to see this sponsored gin post. Alcohol is a depressant that can have a very negative impact on your mental health, so I don't think it should be promoted alongside a mental health hashtag. I appreciate it's an issue that isn't discussed enough, but if you were interested in learning more about it, there are some great accounts you can follow with more information, including @sobergirlsociety.'

For celebrities in particular, Richard from Alcohol Change UK thinks we could draw up a list of those who promote alcohol and then contact them individually and ask them not to.

Share the good stories

Here is what I know from having worked in online journalism. The more clicks a website gets, the more appealing it is for advertisers, and the more money it makes. Unfortunately, stories about the health risks of alcohol will rarely get many hits. On the other hand, a story about how a glass of wine a day could keep the doctor away will no doubt get shared across social media, garnering the website a whole load of clicks, which they can leverage for future advertising deals.

Therefore, publications are more likely to write stories about how wonderful alcohol is for you over why it's not. Now is the time to start sharing the good stories. If you see a magazine post an article about sobriety, tag all your sober friends. If you see a new study about the benefits of cutting back on booze, share it far and wide. If publications can see stories are popular, they'll be more likely to publish similar ones in the future.

Showcase your sobriety

One of the biggest problems we face when it comes to making changes around alcohol harm is the fact that alcohol has been so normalized and ingrained in society that we're at the point where you are considered abnormal if you don't drink. Seeing as we are born sober and alcohol isn't essential for our survival, it's a wonder we've done such a good job of tying it into every single social occasion. This can make it a hard subject to bring up without being thought of as preachy or judgemental.

Essentially, we have a semi-blindness when it comes to alcohol. Sometimes we forget that it's a drug we can live without. We even refer to drugs and alcohol as two separate entities rather than acknowledging that alcohol is a drug. We've embraced a collective denial, and we have sold ourselves the story that drinking is fun and glamorous whereas sober is dull and boring. Now is our chance to change the narrative for good and prove that anything alcohol can do, sobriety can do better.

Most people are like teenagers when talking about drinking – if you tell them they can't do something, they will only want to do it more. Nagging and moaning don't work, they are a waste of your time and energy, and it's not up to you to convince anyone to change their habits.

I have given you the facts about alcohol in this book because you have voluntarily picked it up and I imagine you knew what you were in for, but when it comes to speaking to loved ones, family members and colleagues, I've found that the best approach is to lead by example and sparkle your sober arse off. Glamorizing sobriety and proving that you can live a wonderful hangover-free life is a far quicker way to change the narrative around alcohol and sobriety than bashing booze is.

When it comes to sobriety and activism around alcohol, the choice is yours. Whether you want to scream about the benefits of sobriety from the rooftops, make picket signs about alcohol policy, or simply sit on your sofa and never utter the word 'sober' to a single soul, your decision does not make you any less sober (or incredible). Simply by choosing not to conform to drinking norms, you're as rebellious as they come.

Similarly, if you don't plan to change your drinking after reading this book, it does not make you any less of an amazing human – or a rebel. The fact that you have read to the end of my ramblings is all I could have wished for. I hope whatever happens after this, you make the right decision for you, your health and your happiness, and whether you stick around for good or flit back and forth, you will always be welcome at the Sober Girl Society.

Sober Girl Gains

- [ ] A whole load of new knowledge
- [ ] A use for all those notebooks
- [ ] An activist toolkit
- [ ] A fire in your belly and a reason to rebel
- [ ] A fully fledged membership to the Sober Girl Society

A Final Note

My last gift to you as a welcome to the Sober Girl Society is the final section of this book. Here you will find a non-exhaustive but pretty extensive list of resources to aid you in your sober, sober-curious or mindful-drinking journey. I've included everything mentioned or alluded to in the chapters of this book, but I've also thrown in some extra things for good measure. There are accounts you may want to follow, podcasts you might want to listen to and organizations who can help you – if sobriety had a Yellow Pages, I'd like to think that this would be it.

There are resources that helped me in the early days and things that still help me now because that's the important bit – sobriety is not always easy. We live in a world where alcohol is tied up in every celebration and every commiseration. It starts with 'wetting the baby's head' and ends with a toast to remember that individual's life. This world quite literally revolves around drinking. Until that changes, sobriety is always going to come with its challenges.

But here's the magic, and if you take one thing away from this book let it be this. You are now part of a club, a society, a group of women who are taking back their power and rising up together. We don't have a secret handshake (yet), but we're breaking up with booze and giving hangovers the middle finger. We are living fun, fulfilled lives with clear heads and strong hearts, and we'll be damned if we're going to be held back by alcohol.

Just know that if 'not drinking' ever makes you feel alone, it couldn't be further from the truth. I am so proud of you for being curious, open-minded and questioning things that we have always accepted as the norm. Society tells you that you need to drink to be hilarious, sexy and cool, but at Sober Girl Society we believe that you're already all of those things and so much more.

Remember, alcohol doesn't give you anything wonderful that isn't already inside of you.

All my love,

Millie x

Acknowledgements

Sara, Lauren, Heather, Mel and Taboo – despite the fact that my drunken behaviour has almost killed all of you (and me), you have stuck by me through everything and I couldn't love you more. I'm sorry for all the times I left nightclubs without telling you, all the times you had to convince minicab drivers that I wasn't being sick on the floor, and all the times that we had to go back to bars to retrieve my lost things. I can't believe you're all still my friends.

Emma, Shauna, Leanne, Char, Gabbi and KJ – you are the best cheerleaders a girl could ever ask for. When everything else feels like it's gone to shit, you make everything feel OK. Thank you for your endless support both pre-sobriety and post, celebrating my milestones and entertaining my ideas around organized fun. I can't wait to grow old with you all.

Scott – you were the first friend I made in sobriety and I think someone up there knew I needed you. You're the Little to my Mix. You are outrageously amazing. All my other sober friends, most of whom are mentioned in this book, know you are so very special. There is no feeling more comforting or uplifting than knowing there are people just like you out there, and I will always be grateful for you.

DJ – despite the fact I told you that you wouldn't get a mention in this book, I just couldn't bring myself to leave you out. Though I absolutely managed to keep my cool, I pretty much fell in love with you the minute you offered to do our first date sober. Your open-mindedness to the world and constant enthusiasm is such a rare treasure and I can't believe that I found it by swiping on Bumble. As I like to remind you, this book would absolutely still be here without you, but without your constant love and encouragement, it would have been so much harder to write.

But this book certainly wouldn't be here without the formidable Carly Cook, Lauren Lunn Farrow and Helena Gonda, as well as the amazing Found Entertainment and Transworld teams. Thank you for all believing that the world needed some sober sparkle and that I was the person to sprinkle it.

And lastly to my mum, dad and James (and Magda!). It's not always easy being a Gooch (trying to book restaurants without a snigger is a nightmare), but I wouldn't trade it for the world. I am beyond lucky to have the best parents in the world who I know are utterly relieved they no longer have to call me at 3 a.m. to check that I'm still alive. They say you can't choose your family, but if you could, I'd still pick you.

Support and Resources

All @handles relate to Instagram, and support lines are UK-based

Reading List for the Sober Curious

If your goal is cutting down over quitting, here are a few books that I recommend starting with.

How to be a Mindful Drinker by Club Soda Community
Mindful Drinking by Rosamund Dean
Quit Alcohol (for a Month) by Helen Foster
The 28 Day Alcohol-free Challenge by Andy Ramage and Ruari
  Fairbairns
Sober Curious by Ruby Warrington

Reading List for the Sober Fact-lovers

If you love getting into the neuroscience, want to learn more about addiction or deep-dive into the politics of alcohol, try these titles.

The Easy Way to Control Alcohol by Allen Carr
This Naked Mind by Annie Grace
Chasing the Scream: The Search for the Truth About Addiction by
  Johann Hari

The Biology of Desire: Why Addiction Is Not a Disease by Marc Lewis
In the Realm of Hungry Ghosts: Close Encounters with Addiction
    by Dr Gabor Maté
The Politics of Alcohol by James Nicholls
Drink? The New Science of Alcohol and Your Health by Professor
    David Nutt
Alcohol Explained by William Porter

Reading List for Those Who Like Quit-lit Memoirs

If personal sobriety stories are more your thing, these are the books for you.

Love Yourself Sober by Kate Baily and Mandy Manners
Alcohol Lied to Me by Craig Beck
Sober Positive by Julia Carson
The Sober Survival Guide by Simon Chapple
Drink by Ann Dowsett Johnston
The Unexpected Joy of Being Sober by Catherine Gray
Blackout by Sarah Hepola
The Sober Diaries by Clare Pooley
Girl Walks Out of a Bar by Lisa F. Smith
The Sober Lush by Amanda Eyre Ward and Jardine Libaire
Quit Like a Woman by Holly Whitaker

Sobriety Programmes Mentioned

AA (alcoholics-anonymous.org.uk)
One Year No Beer (oneyearnobeer.com/@oynb)

Smart Recovery (smartrecovery.org.uk)
Tempest (jointempest.com/@jointempest)

Sober Events Mentioned
Day Breaker (daybreaker.com/@dybrkr)
Morning Gloryville (morninggloryville.com/
    @morninggloryville)
Sober and Social (soberandsocial.com/@soberandsocial_)

Books About Crystals
Learn some more about these powerful little stones.

The Crystal Compass by Aisha Amarfio
The Little Book of Crystals by Judy Hall
The Power of Crystal Healing by Emma Lucy Knowles

Sexual Wellness and Masturbation Information
Cherry Revolution (thecherryrevolution.com/
    @cherryrevolution)
Ferly (weareferly.com/@weareferly)
OMGyes (omgyes.com/@omgyesdotcom)

Reading List Outside of Sobriety
Here are some of the books that have helped strengthen my sober resolve by teaching me about other very important things.

Open by Frankie Bridge

Daring Greatly by Brené Brown

Atomic Habits by James Clear

Happy Place by Fearne Cotton

It's Not OK to Feel Blue and Other Lies by Scarlett Curtis

The Art of Happiness by the Dalai Lama

Why I'm No Longer Talking to White People About Race by Reni Eddo-Lodge

Women Don't Owe You Pretty by Florence Given

Mad Girl by Bryony Gordon

Reasons to Stay Alive by Matt Haig

Lost Connections by Johann Hari

Straight Jacket by Matthew Todd

The Power of Now by Eckhart Tolle

Remember This When You're Sad by Maggy Van Eijk

Non-alcoholic Recipe Books

Get mixing and don't forget to send me pictures of your creations.

How to Drink Without Drinking: Celebratory Alcohol-free Drinks for Any Time of the Day by Fiona Beckett

The Seedlip Cocktail Book by Ben Branson

Dry: Non-Alcoholic Cocktails, Cordials and Clever Concoctions by Clare Liardet

Drinking for Two: A Collection of Nutritious Mocktails for the Mom-to-be by Diana Licalzi and Kerry Jane Criss

Redemption Bar: Alcohol-free Cocktails with Benefits by Andrea Waters and Catherine Salway

Sober Podcasts

Whether you listen to them on your daily commute or to wind down before bed, download some of these audio treats. If you're not completely sick of my voice, you'll find interviews with me on some of them.

Hooked: The Unexpected Addicts
Love Sober
Seltzer Squad
Sober Curious
Sober Sips
This Naked Mind

Sober Apps

From tracking your sober days to showing you how much you're saving, sober apps can be really handy!

Club Soda Community
I Am Sober
I'm Done Drinking
Nomo
Pink Cloud
Sober Time
Try Dry

Alcohol-free Venues

Here's a few of the most notable establishments on the sober scene.

Blink Bar: Liverpool, UK
Brewdog AF: London, UK
Café Sobar: Nottingham, UK
Listen Bar: New York City, New York, USA
Redemption Bar: London, UK
Sans Bar: Austin, Texas, USA
Temperance Bar: Los Angeles, California, USA
Virgin Mary Bar: Dublin, Ireland

Sober Girl Spotlights

Where to find the sober mega-babes whose stories you've read in this book.

Africa Brooke (@africabrooke)
Olivia Callaghan (@selfloveliv)
Meg Ellis (@megellisuk)
Laurie McAllister (@laurievmcallister)
Megan Montague (@delightsofmylife)
Lucy Spraggan (@lspraggan)
Ella St John McGrand (@ellastjohnmcgrand)
Emily Syphas (@iamemilysyphas)
Clemmie Telford (@clemmie_telford)

Other Sober Accounts and Communities Mentioned in This Book

If I've included them in these pages, here they are!

Club Soda (@joinclubsoda)

Mel Hamilton (@rebelsobriety)

Love Sober (@lovesober.cic/@mandymannerscoach/
   @katebailycoach)

Proud and Sober (@proudandsober)

Queers Without Beers (@qwb_uk)

Served Up Sober (@servedupsober)

Sober Black Girls Club (@soberblackgirlsclub)

Sober Brown Girls (@soberbrowngirls)

Sober Buzz Scotland (@soberbuzzscotland)

Sober Circle (@sober_circle)

Experts

The wonderful, knowledgeable people I interviewed who answered my questions and contributed their wisdom for this book!

Vicki Anstey (barreworks.co.uk/@vickianstey)

Cate Campbell (catecampbell-psychonatter.com)

Karen J. Gerrard (seamsbeauty.co.uk/@seamsbeauty)

Dorothy Johnson (dorothyabjohnson.com/
   @breakupcoachdorothy)

Dr Jenna Macciochi (drjennamacciochi.com/
   @dr_jenna_macciochi)

Dr Gemma Newman (plantpowerdoctor.com/
   @plantpowerdoctor)
AJ O'Neill (ajoneill.co.uk/@sitdownaj)
Richard Piper (alcoholchange.org.uk/@alcoholchangeuk)
Kristina Sperkova (movendi.ngo)
Amanda White (therapyforwomencenter.com/
   @therapyforwomen)
Rachel Wilson (thegrief.network/@griefnetwork)

More UK Sober Accounts to Follow

Though I haven't been able to squeeze some of them into this
book, here are some wonderful people who brighten my Instagram feed daily.

Joanne Bradford (@motherheart)
Rachel Davies (@rachel_emma_davies)
Catherine Gray (@unexpectedjoyof)
Sammy Hall (@sammy_in_bristol)
Lee Mengo (@thegaysober)
Siobhan O'Connor (@notsosecretlysober)
Sharon Walters (@london_artist1)

International Sober Accounts

We might be separated by the seas but these are some of my
favourite accounts based outside of the UK.

Leah Adam (@bmoreboozeless)
Carly Benson (@carlybbenson)

Rachel Brady (@shotstoshakes)
Allie K. Campbell (@alliekcampbell)
Jen Elizabeth (@resurrektion_of_me)
Es (@sober_otter)
Kelly Fitzgerald Junco (@thesobersenorita)
Lara Frazier (@laraannfrazier)
Emily Gallops (@mysobertravels)
Lindsey Graves (@freeofspirits_)
Amanda Kuda (@authenticallyamanda)
Molly Ruggere (@noglitterinthegutter)
Jolene Park (@healthy_discoveries)
Laura Silverman (@wearesober)

Websites

From personal blogs to websites that publish articles exclusively about sobriety, there's so much evergreen content to find on the web. Here are the ones I look at most.

The Fix (thefix.com)
Girl and Tonic (girlandtonic.co.uk)
Miracles Are Brewing (miraclesarebrewing.com)
Sober Girl Society (obvs!) (sobergirlsociety.com)
The Temper (thetemper.com)

Shops to Buy Non-alcoholic Drinks

Dry Drinker (drydrinker.com)
Wise Bartender (wisebartender.co.uk)
Zeroholic (zeroholic.co.uk)

More Alcohol Charities and Organizations

ADFAM – For families of drug and alcohol users (adfam.org. uk)

Change Grow Live – Specializing in substance misuse and criminal justice intervention projects in England and Wales (changegrowlive.org)

NACOA – National Association for Children of Alcoholics (nacoa.org.uk)

Domestic or Sexual Assault Charities and Helplines

Rape Crisis – Helpline and email support for anyone affected by sexual violence, no matter when or how it happened (rapecrisis.org.uk/0808 8029 999)

Victim Support – Provides specialist practical and emotional support to victims and witnesses of crime (victimsupport.org. uk/0808 1689 111)

The Survivors Trust – Offers support and information to women and girls who have been raped or sexually assaulted (thesurvivorstrust.org/0808 8010 818)

Mental Health Support

Here are some low-cost or free options for support with your mental health. Most colleges and universities will offer free counselling for students who need it, and some employers provide free counselling for their staff via an employee-assistance programme so be sure to ask them if that's an option. Similarly, you can enquire with organizations who train and accredit practitioners. Often they will offer low-cost options with students who are training.

The Blurt Foundation – A social enterprise dedicated to helping those affected by depression (blurtitout.org)

Mind – Advice and support for anyone experiencing mental health problems (mind.org.uk/0300 1233 393)

Papyrus – Young suicide prevention society (papyrus-uk. org/0800 068 4141)

Samaritans – Confidential support for people experiencing feelings of distress or despair (samaritans.org.uk/116 123)

References

1   Gin-dependent Women: Why is alcohol everywhere?

1 'Women: The new market trends in alcohol marketing', European Centre for Monitoring Alcohol Marketing report, 2008 (www.ias.org.uk/uploads/pdf/Women/women_the_new_market_final.pdf).

2 https://eandt.theiet.org/content/articles/2017/11/boozing-britain-suffering-with-waste-and-recycling-headache-research-reveals

3 www.nhs.uk/news/lifestyle-and-exercise/1-5-hospital-patients-have-alcohol-related-problems

2   Independent Women: The curious case of the decline in drinking

1 Fernandez, L., 'One in three people aged 16-24 now "never drink alcohol" and those who do drink less, UCL study finds', *Daily Mail*, 10 October 2018 (www.dailymail.co.uk/health/article-6258559/One-three-aged-16-24-never-drink-alcohol-UCL-study-finds.html).

2 alcoholchange.org.uk/alcohol-facts/fact-sheets/alcohol-statistics

3 Devon, N., 'Sobriety is the new calorie counting and it's becoming toxic', *Stuff*, 7 January 2020 (www.stuff.co.nz/life-style/

well-good/teach-me/118626299/sobriety-is-the-new-calorie-counting-and-its-becoming-toxic).

3   Let's Get Fizzical: Alcohol and your body

1 Markel, H., 'The Last Alcoholic Days of F. Scott Fitzgerald', *JAMA: The Journal of the American Medical Association*, 301(18) (June 2009), 1939–40.

2 Nutt, D., *Drink?: The New Science of Alcohol and Your Health* (London: Yellow Kite, 2020), p. 1.

3 www.education.ninds.nih.gov/brochures/Brain-Basics-Sleep-6-10-08-pdf-508.pdf

4 'IVF couples warned over drinking', *BBC News*, 20 October 2009 (http:news.bbc.co.uk/1/hi/health/8315724.stm).

5 www.nhs.uk/conditions/pregnancy-and-baby/alcohol-medicines-drugs-pregnant

6 www.cancerresearchuk.org/about-cancer/causes-of-cancer/alcohol-and-cancer/does-alcohol-cause-cancer

7 www.nhs.uk/news/food-and-diet/even-moderate-drinking-may-damage-the-brain

8 Nutt, *Drink?*, p. 60

9 Nutt, *Drink?*, p. 58

10 alcoholchange.org.uk/alcohol-facts/fact-sheets/alcohol-statistics; www.alcohol-focus-scotland.org.uk/media/60109/Alcohol-and-young-people-factsheet.pdf

11 'Young mum, 33, dies "after falling down stairs while drunk after five-hour alcohol binge"', *Sun*, 30 September 2018 (www.thesun.co.uk/news/7383713/young-mum-33-dies-drunk-fall-tragic); '"Drunk" British stewardess, 32, just a week into new job died of broken spine from falling down stairs in cabin

when she returned to £6m yacht after night "drinking neat vodka" in Italian Riviera', *Daily Mail*, 22 January 2019 (www. dailymail.co.uk/news/article-6619319/British-stewardess-32-died-breaking-spine-fall-step-cabin.html); 'Drunken student crushed to death in bin lorry, inquest hears', *Guardian*, 7 November 2013 (www.theguardian.com/uk-news/2013/nov/07/drunken-student-garrett-elsey-crushed-death-bin-lorry).

12 Burton, R., and Sheron, N., 'No level of alcohol consumption safe', *Lancet* (published online 23 August 2018) (www.thelancet.com/article/S0140-6736(18)31571-X/fulltext).

13 alcoholchange.org.uk/alcohol-facts/fact-sheets/alcohol-statistics

14 Nutt, *Drink?*, p. 15

15 Knapton, S. 'Three in four people in A&E at weekend are there because of alcohol', *Telegraph*, 21 December 2015 (www. telegraph.co.uk/news/science/science-news/12062056/Three-in-four-people-in-AandE-at-weekend-are-there-because-of-alcohol.html).

4 Sobriety Over Hangxiety: Alcohol and your mind

1 Yao, X. I., et al., 'Change in moderate alcohol consumption and quality of life: evidence from 2 population-based cohorts', *CMAJ*, 191(27) (July 2019), E753–E760 (www.cmaj.ca/content/191/27/E753).

2 Lee, Y. Y., et al., 'Prevalence of binge drinking and its association with mental health conditions and quality of life in Singapore', *Addictive Behaviors*, 100 (January 2020), 106114 (www.sciencedirect.com/science/article/pii/S0306460319304460).

3 Linke, S., and Ussher, M., 'Exercise-based treatments for substance use disorders: evidence, theory, and practicality', *American Journal of Drug and Alcohol Abuse*, 41(1) (January 2015), 7–15 (www.ncbi.nlm.nih.gov/pmc/articles/PMC4831948).

4 University College London, 'Eleven minutes of mindfulness training helps drinkers cut back', *ScienceDaily*, 24 August 2017 (www.sciencedaily.com/releases/2017/08/170824090303.htm).

5 pubmed.ncbi.nlm.nih.gov/25564479/

6 www.ncbi.nlm.nih.gov/pmc/articles/PMC2872355/

5 Get Well Soon: Alcohol and the eight pillars of wellness

1 Dutta, K., 'Average Briton spends £50,000 on alcohol over course of lifetime', *Independent*, 30 September 2014 (www.independent.co.uk/life-style/food-and-drink/news/average-briton-spends-ps50-000-alcohol-over-course-life-time-9763807.html).

6 On Wednesdays We Don't Drink: Friendship, nights out and bottomless brunches

1 Fairbairns, R., 'How to go sober on a stag/hen do and still have an awesome time', *Huffpost* blog, 18 March 2016 (www.huffingtonpost.co.uk/ruari-fairbairns/how-to-go-sober-on-a-stag_b_9459096.html).

2 Ibid.

7 Young Hearts, Rum-free: Romantic relationships and drink-free dating

1 alcoholchange.org.uk/publication/are-you-looking-at-me

8 Let's Talk About (Sober) Sex, Baby: The booze-free birds and the bees

1 Cossar, V., 'One in ten couples haven't made love sober in over six months', *Metro*, 7 August 2013 (metro.co.uk/2013/08/07/one-in-ten-couples-havent-made-love-sober-in-over-six-months-3914874).
2 Gibbons, B., 'Here are the proven benefits of sober sex', *Marie Claire*, 23 November 2016 (www.marieclaire.co.uk/life/sex-and-relationships/sober-sex-441641).
3 www.practicalpainmanagement.com/patient/conditions/headache/treating-migraines-masturbation
4 medicalxpress.com/news/2009-06-vibrator-common-linked-sexual-health.html

9 Soberly Ever After: The hurdles, pitfalls and magical milestones

1 Telfer, N., 'Alcohol and the menstrual cycle', *Clue*, 19 December 2017 (helloclue.com/articles/cycle-a-z/alcohol-cycle).
2 Coldwell, W., 'Did you lose anything at Reading or Leeds festival?', *Guardian*, 25 August 2013 (www.theguardian.com/music/shortcuts/2013/aug/25/lose-anything-reading-leeds-festival).

1 Alcohol Change UK, 'Fit for purpose? An analysis of the role of the Portman Group in alcohol industry self-regulation', July 2018 (https://s3.eu-west-2.amazonaws.com/files.alcoholchange. org.uk/documents/Alcohol_Concern_Alcohol_ResearcH_UK_-_Fit_for_Purpose_-_an_analysis_of_the_role_of_the_Portman_Group.pdf?mtime=20181108131817).

   'A new era for the Portman Group', Portman Group press release, 25 February 2020 (www.portmangroup.org.uk/a-new-era-for-the-portman-group-increased-and-growing-membership).

2 eucam.info/2008/05/06/women-the-new-market/

3 GBD 2016 Alcohol Collaborators, 'Alcohol use and burden for 195 countries and territories, 1990–2016: a systematic analysis for the Global Burden of Disease Study 2016', *Lancet*, 392 (August 2018), 1015–1035 (https://institute.progress.im/en/content/alcohol-consumption-and-its-global-burden-disease).

   Olito, F., 'Alcohol-related deaths have increased dramatically among women, according to a new study', *Insider*, 11 January 2020 (www.insider.com/alcohol-related-deaths-increased-women-research-study-2020-1).

4 alcoholchange.org.uk/alcohol-facts/fact-sheets/alcohol-statistics

5 www.bmj.com/content/369/bmj.m1987

6 www.ias.org.uk/uploads/pdf/News%20stories/balance-report-march2013.pdf

7 www.stonewall.org.uk/lgbt-britain-health

8 orca.cf.ac.uk/58880/

9 Singer, M., *Drugging the Poor: Legal and Illegal Drugs and Social Inequality* (Waveland Press, 2007), p. 128.

10 www.ncbi.nlm.nih.gov/pmc/articles/PMC4455501/

11 alcoholjustice.org/big-alcohol/industry-tactics/19-mar keting-to-target-populations.html

12 realbusiness.co.uk/britains-boozers-fuel-uk-economy-as-alcohol-tax-revenues-top-10bn/

13 candcgroupplc.com/wp-content/uploads/2020/02/CC.FootprintDrinksReport.2020.pdf

14 Buckland, E., 'Rita Ora comes under fire for plugging alcohol on Instagram as campaigners warn celebrity adverts risk "glamourising" underage drinking', *Daily Mail*, 21 May 2019 (www.dailymail.co.uk/tvshowbiz/article-7053273/Rita-Ora-comes-fire-plugging-alcohol-Instagram.html).